saint
of the
Day

A Life and Lesson for Each of the 173 saints of the New Missal

Edited by Leonard Foley, O.F.M.

Nihil Obstat:
     Rev. Hilarion Kistner, O.F.M.
     Rev. John J. Jennings

Imprimi Potest:
     Rev. Roger Huser, O.F.M.
     Provincial

Imprimatur:
     + Joseph L. Bernardin
     Archbishop of Cincinnati
     February 19, 1975

The *Nihil Obstat* and *Imprimatur* are a declaration that a book or pamphlet is considered to be free from doctrinal or moral error. It is not implied that those who have granted the *Nihil Obstat* and *Imprimatur* agree with the contents, opinions, or statements expressed.

Woodcuts by John Quigley, O.F.M. and Stephen D. Kroeger
Cover design by Michael Reynolds

SBN-0-912228-20-2

CONTENTS

iii

AUGUST

SEPTEMBER

iv

DECEMBER

THOMAS, apostle

Poor Thomas! He made one remark and has been branded as "Doubting Thomas" for 20 centuries. But if he doubted, he also believed. He made what is certainly the most explicit statement of faith in the New Testament: "My Lord and my God!" and in so expressing his faith gave Christians a prayer that will be said till the end of time. He also occasioned a compliment from Jesus to us 20th-century Christians: "Thomas, you became a believer because you saw me. Blessed are they who have not seen and have believed."

Thomas should be equally well known for his courage. Perhaps what he said was impetuous —

since he ran, like the rest, at the showdown — but he can scarcely have been insincere when he expressed his willingness to die with Jesus. It was on the occasion when Jesus proposed to go to Bethany when Lazarus had died. Since Bethany was near Jerusalem, this meant walking into the very midst of his enemies, and to almost certain death. Thomas then says to the other apostles, "Let us go along, and die with him."

COMMENT: Thomas shares the lot of Peter the impetuous one, James and John the "sons of thunder," Philip and his foolish question, indeed all the apostles in their weakness, lack of understanding. We must not exaggerate these facts, however, for Christ did not pick worthless men. But their human weakness again points up the fact that holiness is a gift of God, not man's creation; it is given to ordinary men and women with weaknesses; it is God himself who gradually transforms the weaknesses into the image of Christ, the courageous, trusting and loving one.

QUOTE: "Prompted by the Holy Spirit, the Church must walk the same road which Christ walked: a road of poverty and obedience, of service and self-sacrifice to the death. For thus did all the apostles walk in hope. On behalf of Christ's body, the Church, they supplied what was wanting in the sufferings of Christ by their own trials and sufferings" (Vatican II, Missions, 5).

ELIZABETH OF PORTUGAL
(1271-1336)

Elizabeth is usually depicted in royal garb with a dove or an olive branch. At her birth in 1271, her father, Pedro III, future king of Aragon, was reconciled with his father James, the reigning monarch. This proved to be a portent of things to come. Under the healthful influences with which her early years were surrounded, she quickly learned self-discipline and acquired a taste for spirituality. Thus fortunately prepared, she was able to meet the challenge, when at the age of 12, she was given in marriage to Denis, king of Portugal. She was able to establish for herself a pattern of life conducive to growth in God's love, not merely through her exercises of piety, including daily Mass, but also through her exercise of charity, by which she was able to befriend and help pilgrims, strangers, the sick, the poor — in a word all those whose need came to her notice. At the same time she remained devoted to her husband, whose infidelity to her was a scandal to the kingdom.

He too was the object of many of her peace endeavors. She long sought peace for him with God, and was finally rewarded when he gave up his life of sin. She repeatedly sought and effected peace between the king and their rebellious son, Alfonso, who thought that he was passed over to favor the king's illegitimate children. She acted as peacemaker in the struggle between Ferdinand, king of Aragon, and his cousin James, who claimed the crown. And finally from Coimbra, where she had retired as a Franciscan tertiary to the monastery of the Poor Clares after the death of her husband, she set out and was able to bring about a lasting peace between her son Alfonso, now king of Portugal, and his son-in-law, the king of Castile.

COMMENT: The work of promoting peace is anything but a calm and quiet endeavor. It takes a clear mind, a steady spirit, and a brave soul to intervene between men whose emotions are so aroused that they are ready to destroy one another. This is all the more true of a woman in the early 14th century. But Elizabeth had a deep and sincere love and sympathy for mankind, almost a total lack of concern for herself, and an abiding confidence in God. These were the tools of her success.

STORY: Elizabeth was not well enough to undertake her final peacemaking journey, made all the more difficult by the oppressive heat of the season. She would not, however, permit herself to be dissuaded from it. She answered that there was no better way to give of her life and her health than by averting the miseries and destruction of war. By the time she had successfully brought about peace, she was so sick that death was imminent. After her death in 1336, her body was returned to the monastery at Coimbra for burial.

ANTHONY ZACCARIA, priest
(1502-1539)

At the same time that Martin Luther was attacking abuses in the Church, a reformation within the Church was already being attempted. Among the early movers of the Counter-Reformation was Anthony Zaccaria.

His mother became a widow at 18, and devoted herself to the spiritual education of her son. He received a medical doctorate at 22, and while working among the poor of his native Cremona was attracted to the religious apostolate. He renounced his rights to any future inheritance, worked as a catechist, and was ordained priest at the age of 26.

Called to Milan in a few years, he laid the foundations of two religious congregations, one for men, one for women. Their aim was the reform of the decadent society of their day, beginning with the clergy and religious.

Greatly inspired by St. Paul (his congregation is named the Barnabites, after the companion of that saint), he preached with great vigor in church and street, conducted popular missions, and was not ashamed of doing public penance.

He encouraged such innovations as the collaboration of the laity in the apostolate, frequent Communion, the Forty Hours Devotion, and the ringing of church bells at 3:00 p.m. on Fridays.

His holiness moved many to reform their lives; but, as with all saints, it also moved many to oppose him. Twice his community had to undergo official religious investigation, and twice was exonerated.

While on a mission of peace, he became seriously ill and was brought home for a visit to his mother. He died at Cremona at the age of 36.

COMMENT: The austerity of Anthony's spirituality and the Pauline ardor of his preaching would probably "turn off" many people today, as the atrocious phrase puts it. When even some psychiatrists complain at the lack of a sense of sin, it may be time to tell ourselves that not *all* evil is explained by emotional disorder, subconscious and unconscious drives, parental influence, etc. The old-time "hell and damnation" mission sermons have given way to positive, encouraging, biblical homilies. We do indeed need assurance of forgiveness, relief from existential anxiety and future shock. But we still need prophets to stand up and tell us, "He who says he is without sin is a liar."

QUOTE: "In the presence of God and of Christ Jesus, who is coming to judge the living and the dead, and by his appearing and his kingly power, I charge you to preach the word, to stay with this task whether convenient or inconvenient—correcting, reproving, appealing—constantly teaching and never losing patience. For the time will come when people will not tolerate sound doctrine, but, following their own desires, will surround themselves with teachers who tickle their ears" (2 Tim. 4,1-3).

6

MARIA GORETTI, virgin and martyr
(1890-1902)

The largest crowd ever assembled for a canonization — 250,000 — symbolized the reaction of millions touched by the simple story of Maria Goretti.

She was the daughter of a poor Italian tenant-farmer, had no chance to go to school, never learned to read or write. When she made her first Communion, not long before her death at 12, she was one of the larger and somewhat backward members of the class.

On a hot afternoon in July, Mary was sitting at the top of the stairs of her cottage, mending a shirt. She was not quite 12 years old, but physically mature. A cart stopped outside, and a neighbor, Alessandro, 18 years old, ran up the stairs. He seized her and pulled her into a bedroom. She struggled and tried to call for help, gasping that she would be killed rather than submit. "No, God does not wish it. It is a sin. You would go to hell for it." Alessandro began striking at her blindly with a long dagger.

She was taken to a hospital. Her last hours were marked by the usual simple compassion of the good — concern about where her mother would sleep, forgiveness of her murderer (she had been in fear of him, but did not say anything lest she cause trouble to his family) and her devout welcoming of Viaticum. She died about 24 hours after the attack.

Her murderer was sentenced to 30 years in

prison. For a long time he was unrepentant and surly. One night he had a dream or vision of Maria, gathering flowers and offering them to him. His life changed. When he was released after 27 years, his first act was to go to beg the forgiveness of Maria's mother.

Devotion to the young martyr grew, miracles were worked, and in less than a half-century she was canonized. At her beatification in 1947, her mother (then 82), two sisters and a brother appeared with Pope Pius XII on the balcony of St. Peter's. Three years later, at her canonization, a 66-year-old Alessandro Serenelli knelt among the quarter-million people and cried tears of joy.

COMMENT: Maria may have had trouble with catechism, but she had no trouble with faith. God's will was holiness, decency, respect for one's body, absolute obedience, total trust. In a complex world, her faith was simple: It is a privilege to be loved by God, and to love him — at any cost. As the virtue of chastity dies the death of a thousand qualifications, she is a breath of sweet fresh air.

QUOTE: "Even if she had not been a martyr, she would still have been a saint, so holy was her everyday life" (Cardinal Salotti).

BENEDICT, abbot
(480?-543)

It is unfortunate that no contemporary biography was written of a man who has exercised measureless influence on monasticism in the West. Benedict is well recognized in the later *Dialogues* of St. Gregory, but these are sketches to illustrate miraculous elements of his career.

He was born of a distinguished family in central Italy, studied at Rome, and early in life was drawn to the monastic life. At first he became a hermit, leaving a depressing world — pagan armies on the march, the Church torn by schism, people suffering from war, morality at a low ebb.

He soon realized that he could not live a hidden life in a small town any better than in a large city, so he withdrew to a cave high in the mountains for three years. Some monks chose him as their leader for a while, but found his strictness not to their taste. Still, the shift from hermit to community life had begun for him. He had an idea of gathering various families of monks into one "Grand Monastery" to give them the benefit of unity, fraternity, permanent worship in one house. Finally he began to build what was to become one of the most famous monasteries in the world — Monte Cassino, commanding three narrow valleys running toward the mountain.

The rule that gradually developed prescribed a life of liturgical prayer, study, manual labor, and living together in community under a common father (abbot). Benedictine asceticism is known for its moderation, and Benedictine charity has always shown concern for the people in the surrounding countryside. In the course of the Middle Ages, all monasticism in the West was gradually brought under the rule of St. Benedict.

Today the Benedictine family is represented by two branches: the Benedictine Federation and the Cistercians.

The feast of Benedict's sister, Scholastica, is celebrated February 10.

COMMENT: The Church has been blessed through Benedictine devotion to the liturgy, not only in its actual celebration with rich and proper ceremony in the great abbeys, but also through the scholarly studies of many of its members. Liturgy is sometimes confused with guitars, balloons, Latin or Bach. We should be grateful to those who both preserve and adapt the genuine tradition of worship in the Church.

QUOTE: "Rightly, then, the liturgy is considered as an exercise of the priestly office of Jesus Christ. In the liturgy the sanctification of man is manifested by signs perceptible to the senses . . . . In the liturgy full public worship is performed by the Mystical Body of Jesus Christ, that is, by the Head and his members.

From this it follows that every liturgical celebration, because it is an action of Christ the priest and of his Body the Church, is a sacred action, surpassing all others" (Vatican II, Liturgy, 7).

HENRY
(972-1024)

As German king and Roman Emperor, Henry was a practical man of affairs. He was energetic in consolidating his rule. He crushed rebellions and feuds. On all sides he had to deal with drawn-out disputes so as to protect his frontiers. This involved him in a number of battles, especially in the south in Italy; he also helped Pope Benedict VIII quell disturbances in Rome. Always his ultimate purpose was to establish a stable peace in Europe.

According to 11th-century custom, Henry took advantage of his position and filled bishoprics with men loyal to him. In his case, however, he avoided the pitfalls of this practice and actually fostered the reform of ecclesiastical and monastic life.

COMMENT: All in all, this saint was a man of his times. From our standpoint, he may have been too quick to do battle and too ready to use power to accomplish reforms. But, granted such limitations, he shows that holiness is possible in a busy secular life. It is in doing our job that we become saints.

QUOTE: "We deem it opportune to remind our children of their duty to take an active part in public life and to contribute toward the attainment of the common good of the entire human family as well as to that of their own political community. They should endeavor, therefore, in the light of their Christian faith and led by love, to insure that the various institutions — whether economic, social, cultural or political in purpose — should be such as not to create obstacles, but rather to facilitate or render less arduous man's perfecting of himself in both the natural order and the supernatural . . . . Every believer in this world of ours must be a spark of light, a center of love, a vivifying leaven amidst his fellow men. And he will be this all the more perfectly, the more closely he lives in communion with God in the intimacy of his own soul" (Pope John XXIII, *Pacem in Terris,* Nos. 146 and 164).

July 14   *Optional*

CAMILLUS de LELLIS, priest
(1550-1614)

Humanly speaking, Camillus was not a likely candidate for sainthood. His mother died when he was a child, his father neglected him, and he grew up with an excessive love for gambling. At 17 he was afflicted with a disease of his leg that remained with him for life. In Rome, he entered the San Giacomo hospital for incurables as both patient and servant, but was dismissed for quarrelsomeness after nine months. He served in the Venetian army for three years. Then, in the winter of 1574, when he was 24, he gambled away everything he had — savings, weapons, literally down to his shirt. He accepted work at the Capuchin friary at Manfredonia, and was one day so moved by a sermon of the superior that he began a conversion that changed his whole life. He entered the Capuchin novitiate, but was dismissed because of the apparently incurable sore on his leg. After another stint of service at San Giacomo, he came back to the Capuchins, only to be dismissed again, for the same reason.

Again back at San Giacomo, his dedication was rewarded by his being made superintendent. He devoted the rest of his life to the care of the sick, and has been named, along with St. John of God, patron of hospitals, nurses and the sick. With the advice of his friend St. Philip Neri, he studied for the priesthood and was ordained at the age of 34. Contrary to the advice of his friend, he left San Giacomo and founded a congregation of his own. As superior, he devoted much of his own time to the care of the sick.

Charity was his first concern, but the physical aspects of the hospital also received his diligent attention. He insisted on cleanliness and the technical competence of those who served the sick. The members of his community bound themselves to serve prisoners and persons infected by the plague as well as those dying in private homes. Some of his men were with troops fighting in Hungary and Croatia in 1595, forming the first recorded military field ambulance. In Naples, he and his men went onto the galleys that had plague and were not allowed to land. He discovered that there were people being buried alive, and ordered his brothers to continue the prayers for the dying 15 minutes after apparent death.

He himself suffered the disease of his leg through his life. In his last illness he left his own bed to see if other patients in the hospital needed help.

COMMENT: Saints are created by God. Parents must indeed nurture the faith in their children; husbands and wives must cooperate to deepen their baptismal grace; friends must support each other. But all human effort is only the dispensing of divine power. We must all "try" as if everything depended on us. But only the power of God can fulfill the plan of God — to make us like himself.

STORY: A doctor in Philadelphia is a modern Camillus. An AP news story reports that the 31-year-old bachelor does not have an office, and gave up a lucrative health center job to treat the chronically ill in the inner city who cannot get to a clinic. He limits his practice to house calls in the ghetto.

July 15   *Memorial*

BONAVENTURE, bishop and doctor
(1221-1274)

Bonaventure, Franciscan, theologian, doctor of the Church, was both learned and holy. Because of the spirit that filled him and his writings, he was at first called the Devout Doctor; but in more recent centuries he has been known as the Seraphic Doctor, because of the truly Franciscan spirit he possessed.

Born in Bagnoregio, a town in central Italy, he was cured of a serious illness as a boy through the prayers of Francis of Assisi. Later, he studied the arts at Paris. Inspired by Francis and the example of

14

the friars, especially of his master in theology, Alexander of Hales, he entered the Franciscan Order, and became in turn a teacher of theology in the University. Chosen as General of the order in 1257, he was God's instrument in bringing the Order back to a deeper love of the way of St. Francis, both through the life of Francis which he wrote at the behest of the brothers, and through other works in defense of the Order or in explanation of its ideals and way of life.

COMMENT: Bonaventure so united holiness and theological knowledge that he rose to the heights of mysticism while yet remaining a very active preacher and teacher, one beloved by all who met him. To know him was to love him; to read him is still for us today to meet a true Franciscan and a gentleman.

STORY: The morning of the 15th of July, 1274, in the midst of the Second Council of Lyons, Pope Gregory X and the Fathers of the Council were shocked to learn that toward dawn Brother Bonaventure, bishop of Albano, had sickened and died. An unknown chronicler provides his impression of the Franciscan cardinal: "A man of eminent learning and eloquence, and of outstanding holiness, he was known for his kindness, approachableness, gentleness and compassion. Full of virtue, he was beloved of God and man. At his funeral Mass that same day, many were in tears, for the Lord had granted him this grace, that whoever came to know him was forthwith drawn to a deep love of him."

LAWRENCE OF BRINDISI,
priest and doctor
(1559-1619)

At first glance perhaps the most remarkable quality of Lawrence of Brindisi is his outstanding gift of languages. In addition to a thorough knowledge of his native Italian, he had a complete reading and speaking ability in Latin, Hebrew, Greek, German, Bohemian, Spanish and French.

He was born on July 22, 1559, and died exactly 60 years later on his birthday in 1619. His parents William and Elizabeth Russo gave him the name of Julius Caesar, or "Caesare" in Italian. After the early death of his parents he was educated by his uncle at the College of St. Mark in Venice.

When he was just 16 he entered the Capuchin Franciscan Order in Venice, and he received the new name of Lawrence. He completed his studies of philosophy and theology at the University of Padua and was ordained a priest at 23.

With his facility for languages he was able to study the Bible in its original texts. At the request of Pope Clement VIII he spent much time preaching to the Jews in Italy. So excellent was his knowledge of Hebrew, the rabbis felt sure he was a Jew who had become a Christian.

The Capuchin Order completed a compilation of 15 volumes of his writings in 1956. Eleven of these 15 contain his sermons, each of which relies chiefly on scriptural quotations to illustrate his teaching.

A character trait surfaced — perhaps not expected in such a talented scholar — which indicated Lawrence's sensitivity to the needs of people. He was elected major superior of the Capuchin Franciscan Province of Tuscany at the age of 31. He had the combination of brilliance, human compassion, and administrative skill needed to carry out his duties. In rapid succession he was promoted by his fellow Capuchins and was elected Minister General of the entire Order in 1602. In this position he was responsible for great growth and geographical expansion of the Order.

Lawrence was appointed Papal Emissary and peacemaker, a job which took him to a number of foreign countries. An effort to achieve peace in his native kingdom of Naples took him on a journey to Lisbon to visit the king of Spain. Serious illness in Lisbon took his life in 1619.

COMMENT: His constant devotion to Scripture, coupled with great sensitivity to the needs of people, present a life-style which appeals to 20th-century Christians. Lawrence had a balance in his life that was able to blend self-discipline with a keen appreciation for the needs of those whom he was called to serve.

QUOTE: *Scotist Teaching on the Primacy of Christ:* "God is love, and all his operations proceed from love. Once he wills to manifest that goodness by sharing his love outside himself, then the Incarnation becomes the supreme manifestation of his goodness and love and glory. So, Christ was intended before all other creatures and for his own sake. For him all things were created and to him all things must be subject, and God loves all creatures in and because of Christ. Christ is the first-born of every creature, and the whole of humanity as well as the created world finds its foundation and meaning in him. Moreover, this would have been the case even if Adam had not sinned" *(St. Lawrence of Brindisi, Doctor of the Universal Church,* Capuchin Educational Conference, Washington, D.C.).

July 22   *Memorial*

MARY MAGDALEN

Except for the mother of Jesus, few women are more honored in the Bible than Mary Magdalen. Yet she could well be the patron of the slandered, since there has been a persistent legend in the Church that she is the unnamed sinful woman of Luke 7,36 who anointed the feet of Jesus.

Most Scripture scholars today point out that there is no scriptural basis for confusing the two. Mary Magdalen, i.e., "of Magdala" was the one from whom Christ cast out "seven devils," — an indication, at the worst, of extreme demonic possession; or possibly severe illness.

Father W. J. Harrington, O.P., writing in the *New Catholic Commentary,* says that "seven devils" "does not mean that Mary had lived an immoral life — a conclusion reached only by means of a mistaken identification with the anonymous woman of Luke 7,36." Father Edward Mally, S.J., writing in the

Jerome Biblical Commentary, agrees that she "is not . . . the same as the sinner of Luke 7,37, despite the later Western romantic tradition about her."

Mary Magdalen was one of the many "who were assisting them (Jesus and the Twelve) out of their means." She was one of those who stood by the cross of Jesus with his mother. And, of all the "official" witnessess that might have been chosen for the first awareness of the resurrection, she was the one to whom that privilege was given.

COMMENT: Mary Magdalen has been smiling at her "mistaken identity" for 19 centuries. Yet she would no doubt insist that it makes no difference. We are all sinners in need of the saving power of God, whether our sins have been lurid or not. More importantly, we are all, with her, "unofficial" witnesses of the resurrection.

STORY: Today's Gospel (John 20, 1-2. 11-18) shows Mary at first not recognizing the risen Jesus in the garden, then knowing him as he spoke her name. Her great love bursts forth (First reading, Canticle of Canticles, 3,1-4: "I took hold of him and would not let him go"). Jesus says, "Do not cling to me, (or "Do not attempt to touch me,") for I have not yet ascended to the Father." The meaning probably is that there is an entirely new relationship now — a much deeper one, resting in faith, rather than the former relationship that was possible because of his visible body. St. John may also be stressing the fact that Jesus' exaltation at the right hand of the Father is the completion of the resurrection.

At first, the apostles did not believe her. Christ's

followers, even today, meet disbelief in their witness to the resurrection

BRIDGET, religious
(1303?-1373)

From age seven on, Bridget had visions of Christ crucified. Her visions formed the basis for her activity — always with the value on charity rather than spiritual favors.

She lived her married life in the court of the Swedish king, Magnus the Second. Mother of eight children, (the second eldest was St. Catherine of Sweden), she lived the strict life of a penitent after her husband's death.

Bridget constantly strove to exert her good influence over Magnus; and while never fully reforming, he did give her land and buildings to found a monastery for men and women. This group eventually expanded into an order known as the Bridgettines (still in existence).

In 1350, a year of jubilee, Bridget braved a plague-stricken Europe to make a pilgrimage to Rome. She never returned to Sweden, and her years in Rome were far from happy, being hounded by debts and opposition to her work against Church abuses.

A final pilgrimage to the Holy Land, marred by shipwreck and the death of her son, Charles, eventually led to her death in 1373.

COMMENT: Bridget's visions, rather than isolating her from the affairs of the world, involved her in many contemporary issues, whether they be royal policy or the Avignon papacy. She saw no contradiction between mystical experience and secular activity, and her life is a testimony to the possibility of a holy life in the market place.

QUOTE: Despite the hardships of life and wayward children (not all became saints), Margery Kempe of Lynn says Bridget was "kind and meek to every creature" and "she had a laughing face."

July 25   *Feast*

JAMES, apostle

This James is the brother of John the Evangelist. The two were called by Jesus as they worked with their father in a fishing boat on the Sea of Galilee. Jesus had already called another pair of brothers from a similar occupation: Peter and Andrew. "Going on a little farther, he saw James the son of Zebedee and his brother John; they also were in their boat mending their nets. Immediately he called them, and they left their father Zebedee in the boat with the hired men, and followed him."

James was one of the favored three who had the privilege of witnessing the Transfiguration, the raising to life of the daughter of Jairus, and the Agony in Gethsemane.

Two incidents in the Gospels describe the temperament of this man and his brother. St. Matthew

21

tells that their mother came (Mark says it was the brothers themselves) to ask that they have the seats of honor (one on the right, one on the left of Jesus) in the kingdom. Jesus said, "You don't know what you are asking for! Can you drink of the cup of which I will drink, or be baptized with the baptism with which I am to be baptized?" They answered, "We can." Jesus then told them they would drink the cup and share his baptism of pain and death, but that sitting at his right hand or left was not his to give — it is "for those to whom it has been reserved by the Father." It remained to be seen how long it would take to realize the implications of their confident "We can!"

The other disciples became indignant at the ambition of James and John. Then Jesus taught them all the lesson of humble service: the purpose of authority is to serve. They are not to impose their will on others, or lord it over them. This is the position of Jesus himself. He was the servant of all; the service imposed on him was the supreme sacrifice of his own life.

On another occasion, James and John gave evidence that the nickname Jesus gave them — "sons of thunder" — was an apt one. The Samaritans would not welcome Jesus because he was on his way to hated Jerusalem. "When his disciples James and John saw this, they said, 'Lord, would you not have us call down fire from heaven to destroy them?' He turned toward them only to reprimand them."

James was apparently the first of the apostles to be martyred. "During that period, King Herod started to harass some of the members of the Church.

22

He beheaded James, the brother of John, and when he saw that this pleased certain of the Jews, he took Peter into custody also."

This James is not to be confused with the author of the Letter of James, or with the leader of the Jerusalem community.

COMMENT: The way the Gospels treat the apostles is a good reminder of what holiness is all about. There is very little about their virtues as static possessions whereby they would have some title to heavenly reward. Rather, the great emphasis is on the Kingdom, on God's giving them the power to witness personally to Jesus' presence, to heal, to proclaim the Good News. As far as their personal lives are concerned, there is much about Jesus' purifying them of narrowness, pettiness, fickleness.

QUOTE: "Christ the Lord, in whom the full revelation of the supreme God is brought to completion, commissioned the apostles to preach to all men that gospel which is the source of all saving truth and moral teaching, and thus to impart to them divine gifts. This commission was faithfully fulfilled by the apostles, who, by their oral preaching, by example, and by ordinances, handed on what they had received from the lips of Christ, from living with him, and from what he did, or what they had learned through the promptings of the Holy Spirit" (Vatican II, Revelation, 7).

JOACHIM and ANN,
parents of Mary

In the Scriptures, Matthew and Luke furnish a legal family history of Jesus, tracing ancestry to show that Jesus is the culmination of great promises. His mother's family is not only neglected, but we know nothing factual about them except that they existed. Even the names of Joachim and Ann come from a legendary source written more than a century after Jesus died.

The heroism and holiness of these people, however, is inferred from the whole family atmosphere around Mary in the Scriptures. Whether we rely on the legends about Mary's childhood or make guesses from the information in the Bible, we see in her a fulfillment of many generations of prayerful persons, herself steeped in the religious traditions of her people.

The strong character of Mary in making decisions, her continuous practice of prayer, her devotion to the laws of her faith, her steadiness at moments of crisis, and her devotion to her relatives — all indicate a close-knit, loving family that looked forward to the next generation even while retaining the best of the past.

Joachim and Ann — whether this is their real name or not — represent that entire quiet series of generations who faithfully perform their duties, practice their faith, and establish an atmosphere for the coming of the Messiah, but remain obscure.

COMMENT: This is the "feast of grandparents." It reminds grandparents of their responsibility to establish a tone for generations to come: they must make the traditions live and offer them as a promise to little children. But the feast has a message for the younger generation as well. It reminds the young that older people's greater perspective, depth of experience, and appreciation of life's profound rhythms are all part of a wisdom not to be taken lightly or ignored.

QUOTE: "The family is the foundation of society. In it the various generations come together and help one another to grow wise and to harmonize personal rights with the other requirements of social life" (Vatican II, The Church in the Modern World, 52).

July 29   *Memorial*

MARTHA

Martha, Mary and their brother Lazarus were evidently close friends of Jesus. He came to their home simply as a welcome guest, rather than as one celebrating the conversion of a sinner (Zacchaeus) or as one unceremoniously received by a suspicious Pharisee. The sisters feel free to call on Jesus at their brother's death, even though a return to Judea at that time seemed almost certain death.

No doubt Martha was an active sort of person: she prepares the meal for Jesus and possibly his fellow guests, and forthrightly states the obvious: all hands should pitch in to help with the dinner.

Yet, as Father John McKenzie points out, she need not be rated as an "unrecollected activist." The evangelist is emphasizing what our Lord said on several occasions about the primacy of the spiritual: "Do not worry about what you are to eat or drink . . . . Seek first his kingship over you"; "Not on bread alone . . . ."; "Blessed are they who hunger and thirst after holiness."

Martha's great glory is her simple and strong statement of faith in Jesus at the time of her brother's death. Jesus said, "I am the resurrection and the life:

whoever believes in me, though he should die, will come to life; and whoever is alive and believes in me, will never die. Do you believe this?" Martha replied, "Yes, Lord, I have come to believe that you are the Messiah, the Son of God: he who is to come into the world."

COMMENT: Scripture commentators point out that in writing his account of the raising of Lazarus, St. John intends that we should see Martha's words to Mary before the resurrection of Lazarus as a summons that every Christian must obey. In her saying "The Master is here and calls for you," Jesus is calling every one of us to resurrection — now in baptismal faith, forever in our sharing his victory over death. And each of us, in our own unique way, is called to special friendship with him as were these three friends.

QUOTE: "Even in this life the Spirit transforms us . . . . When Moses turned towards the Lord, his face shone with the reflection of God; when the believer turns towards the Lord Jesus and contemplates his glorious face, he is transformed into an ever brighter image of that same glory. And the irradiating power which transforms us into beings of light only comes from Christ because he himself is wholly penetrated by that Spirit" (Durrwell, *The Resurrection,* p. 97).

PETER CHRYSOLOGUS,
bishop and doctor
(406-450?)

A man who vigorously pursues a goal may produce results far beyond his expectations and his intentions. Thus it was with Peter of the Golden Words, as he was called, who as a young man became Bishop of Ravenna, the capital of the empire in the West. At the time there were abuses and vestiges of paganism evident in his diocese, and these he was determined to battle and overcome. His principal weapon was the short sermon, and many of them have come down to us. It is readily understandable that such sermons do not contain great originality of thought. They are, however, full of moral applications, sound in doctrine, and historically significant in that they reveal Christian life in fifth-century Ravenna. So authentic were the contents of his sermons that some 13 centuries later, he was declared a doctor of the Church by Pope Benedict XIII. He who had earnestly sought to teach and motivate his own flock was recognized as a teacher of the universal Church.

In addition to his zeal in the exercise of his office, Peter Chrysologus was distinguished by a fierce loyalty to the Church, not only in her teaching, but in her authority as well. He looked upon learning not as a mere opportunity but as an obligation for all, both as a development of God-given faculties and as a solid support for the worship of God.

Some time before his death, St. Peter returned to Imola, his birthplace, where he died c. 450 A.D.

COMMENT: Quite likely, it was St. Peter Chrysologus' attitude toward learning that gave substance to his exhortations. Next to virtue, learning, in his view, was the greatest improver of the human mind and the support of true religion. Ignorance is not a virtue, nor is anti-intellectualism. Knowledge is neither more nor less a source of pride than physical, administrative or financial prowess. To be fully human is to expand our knowledge — whether sacred or secular — according to our talent and opportunity.

STORY: Eutyches, the leader of the heresy denying the humanity of Christ, sought support from Church leaders, Peter Chrysologus among them, after his condemnation in 448 A.D. Peter frankly told him: "In the interest of peace and the faith, we cannot judge in matters of faith, without the consent of the Roman bishop." He further exhorted Eutyches to accept the mystery of the Incarnation in simple faith. Peter reminded him that if the peace of the Church causes joy in heaven, then divisions must give birth to grief.

July 31   *Memorial*

IGNATIUS OF LOYOLA, priest
(1491-1556)

The founder of the Jesuits was on his way to military fame and fortune when a cannonball shattered his leg. Because there were no books of romance on hand during his convalescence, he whiled away the time reading a life of Christ and lives of the saints. His conscience was deeply touched, and a long, painful turning to Christ began. Having seen the Mother of God in a vision, he made a pilgrimage to her shrine at Monserrat. He remained for almost a year at nearby Manresa, sometimes with the Dominicans, sometimes in a pauper's hospice, often in a cave in the hills praying. After a period of great peace of mind, he went through a harrowing trial of scruples. There was no comfort in anything — prayer, fasting, sacraments, penance. At length, his peace of mind returned.

It was during this year of conversion that he began to write down material that later became his greatest work, the *Spiritual Exercises.*

He finally achieved his purpose of going to the Hold Land, but could not remain, as he planned, because of the hostility of the Turks. He spent the next 11 years in various European universities, studying with great difficulty, beginning almost as a child. Like many others, he fell victim twice to the suspicions of the time, and was twice jailed for brief periods.

In 1534, at the age of 33, he and six others (one of whom was Francis Xavier) vowed to live in poverty and chastity and to go to the Holy Land. If this became impossible, they vowed to offer themselves to the apostolic service of the Pope. The latter became the only choice. Four years later Ignatius made the association permanent. The new Society of Jesus was approved by Paul III, and Ignatius was elected to serve as the first general.

When companions were sent on various missions by the Pope, Ignatius remained in Rome, consolidating the new venture, but still finding time to found homes for orphans, catechumens and penitents. He founded the Roman College, intended to be the model of all other colleges of the Society.

Ignatius was a true mystic. He centered his spiritual life on the essential foundations of Christianity — the Trinity, Christ, the Eucharist. His spirituality is expressed in the Jesuit motto, *ad majorem Dei gloriam* — "for the greater glory of God." In his concept, obedience was to be the prominent virtue, to assure the effectiveness and mobility of his men. All activity was to be guided by a true love of the Church and unconditional obedience to the Holy Father, for which reason all professed members took a fourth vow to go wherever the Pope should send them for the salvation of souls.

COMMENT: Luther nailed his theses to the church door at Wittenberg in 1517. Seventeen years later, Ignatius founded the Society that was to play so prominent a part in the Counter-Reformation. He was an implacable foe of Protestantism. Yet the seeds of ecumenism may be found in his words! "Great care must be taken to show forth orthodox truth in such a way that if any heretics happen to be present they may have an example of charity and Christian moderation. No hard words should be used nor any sort of contempt for their errors be shown." One of the greatest figures in the modern ecumenical movement was Cardinal Bea, a Jesuit.

QUOTE: He recommended this prayer to penitents: "Receive, Lord, all my liberty, my memory, my understanding and my whole will. You have given me all that I have, all that I am, and I surrender all to your divine will, that you dispose of me. Give me only your love and your grace. With this I am rich enough, and I have no more to ask."

ALPHONSUS LIGUORI,
bishop and doctor
(1696-1787)

Moral theology, Vatican II said, should be more thoroughly nourished by Scripture, and show the nobility of the Christian vocation of the faithful, and their obligation to bring forth fruit in charity for the life of the world. Alphonsus, declared patron of moral theologians by Pius XII in 1950, would rejoice in that statement. In his day, he fought for the liberation of moral theology from the rigidity of Jansenism. His moral theology, which went through 60 editions in the century following him, concentrated on the practical and concrete problems of pastors and confessors. If a certain legalism and minimalism crept into moral theology, it should not be attributed to this model of moderation and gentleness.

At the University of Naples he received, at the age of 16, a doctorate in both canon and civil law, by acclamation, but soon gave up the practice of law for apostolic activity. He was ordained priest and concentrated his pastoral efforts on popular (parish) missions, hearing confessions, forming of Christian groups.

He founded the Redemptorist congregation in 1732. It was an association of priests and brothers living a common life, dedicated to the imitation of Christ, and working mainly in popular missions for peasants in rural areas. Almost as an omen of what was to come later, he found himself deserted, after a while, by all his original companions except one lay brother. But the congregation managed to survive and was formally approved 17 years later, though its troubles were not over.

Alphonsus' great pastoral reforms were in pulpit and confessional — replacing the pompous oratory of the time with simplicity, and the rigorism of Jansenism with kindness. His great fame as writer has somewhat eclipsed the fact that for 26 years he traveled up and down the kingdom of Naples preaching popular missions.

He was made bishop (after trying to reject the honor) at 66 and at once instituted a thorough reform of the diocese.

The end of his life witnessed his greatest sorrow. The Redemptorists, precariously continuing after the suppression of the Jesuits, had difficulty in getting their rule approved by the Kingdom of Naples. Alphonsus acceeded to the condition that they possess no property in common, but a royal official, with the connivance of a high Redemptorist official, changed the rule substantially. Alphonsus, old, crippled and with very bad sight, signed the document, unaware that he had been betrayed. The

Redemptorists in the Papal States then put themselves under the Pope, who withdrew those in Naples from the jurisdiction of Alphonsus. It was only after his death that the branches were united.

At 71 he was afflicted with rheumatic pains which left incurable bending of his neck; until it was straightened a little, the pressure of his chin caused a raw wound on his chest. He suffered a final 18 months of "dark night" scruples, fears, temptations against every article of faith and every virtue, interspersed with intervals of light and relief, when ecstasies were frequent.

Alphonsus is best known for his moral theology, but also wrote well in the field of spiritual and dogmatic theology. His *Glories of Mary* is one of the great works on that subject, and his book *Visits to the Blessed Sacrament* went through 40 editions in his lifetime, greatly influencing the practice of this devotion in the Church.

COMMENT: St. Alphonsus was known above all as a practical man who dealt in the concrete rather than the abstract. His life is indeed a "practical" model for the everyday Christian who has difficulty recognizing the dignity of Christian life amid the swirl of problems, pain, misunderstanding and failure. Alphonsus suffered all these things. He is a saint because he was able to maintain an intimate sense of the presence of the suffering Christ through it all.

QUOTE: Someone once remarked, after a sermon by Alphonsus, "It is a pleasure to listen to your sermons; you forget yourself and preach Jesus Christ."

EUSEBIUS OF VERCELLI, bishop
(283?-371)

Someone has said that if there had been no Arian heresy it would be very difficult to write the lives of many early saints. Eusebius is another of the defenders of the Church during one of its most trying periods.

Born on the isle of Sardinia, he became a member of the Roman clergy and is the first recorded bishop of Vercelli in Piedmont. He is also the first to join the monastic life with that of the clergy, establishing a community of his diocesan clergy on the principle that the best way to sanctify his people was to have them see a clergy formed in solid virtue and living in community.

He was sent by Pope Liberius to persuade the emperor to call a council to settle Catholic-Arian troubles. When it was called at Milan, Eusebius went reluctantly, sensing that the Arian block would have its way though the Catholics were more numerous. He refused to go along with the condemnation of Athanasius; instead, he laid the Nicene creed on the table and insisted that all sign it before taking up any other matter. The Emperor put pressure on him, but Eusebius insisted on Athanasius' innocence and reminded the emperor that secular force should not be used to influence Church decisions. At first the emperor threatened to kill him, but later sent him into exile in Palestine. There the Arians dragged him through the streets and shut him up in a little room, releasing him only after his four-day hunger strike, but continuing their harassment shortly after.

His exile continued in Asia Minor and Egypt, until the new emperor permitted him to be welcomed back to his see in Vercelli. He attended the Council of Alexandria with Athanasius and approved the leniency shown to bishops who had wavered. He also worked with St. Hilary of Poitiers against the Arians.

He died peacefully in his own diocese at an advanced age.

COMMENT: Catholics in the U.S. have sometimes felt penalized by an unwarranted interpretation of the principle of separation of Church and state, especially in the matter of Catholic schools. Be that as it may, the Church is happily free today from the tremendous pressure put on it after its becoming an "established" Church under Constantine. We are happily rid of such things as a pope asking an emperor to call a Church council, Pope John I being sent by the emperor to negotiate in the East, the pressure of kings on papal elections. The Church cannot be a prophet if it's in anybody's pocket.

QUOTE: "To render the care of souls more efficacious, community life for priests is strongly recommended, especially for those attached to the same parish. While this way of living encourages apostolic action, it also affords an example of charity and unity to the faithful" (Vatican II, Bishops, 30).

JOHN VIANNEY, priest
(1786-1859)

A man with vision overcomes obstacles and performs deeds that seem impossible. John Vianney was a man with vision: he wanted to become a priest. But he had to overcome his meager formal schooling which did not equip him adequately for seminary studies.

His failure to comprehend Latin lectures forced him to discontinue. But his vision of being a priest urged him to seek private tutoring. After a lengthy battle with the books, John was ordained.

Situations calling for "impossible" deeds followed him everywhere. As pastor of the parish at Ars, John encountered people who were indifferent and quite comfortable with their style of living. His vision lead him through severe fasts and short nights of sleep. "Some devils can only be cast out by prayer and fasting."

With Catherine Lassagne and Benedicta Lardet, he established La Providence, a home for girls. Only a man of vision could have such trust that God would provide for the spiritual and material needs of all those who came to make La Providence their home.

His work as a confessor is John Vianney's most remarkable accomplishment. In the winter months he was to spend 11 to 12 hours daily reconciling people with God. In summer months this time was increased to 16 hours. Unless a man was dedicated to his vision of a priestly vocation, he could not have endured this giving of self day after day.

Many people look forward to retirement and taking it easy, doing the things they always wanted to do but never had the time for. But John Vianney had no thoughts of retirement. As his fame spread, more hours were consumed in serving God's people. Even the few hours he would allow himself for sleep were disturbed frequently by the devil.

Who, but a man with vision, could keep going with ever-increasing strength?

COMMENT: Indifference toward religion, coupled with a love for material comfort, seem to be common signs of our times. If a person from another planet would observe us, it is unlikely he would judge us to be pilgrim people, on our way to somewhere else. John Vianney, on the other hand, was a man on a journey with his goal before him at all times.

QUOTE: Recommending liturgical prayer, John Vianney would say, "Private prayer is like straw scattered here and there: if you set it on fire it makes a lot of little flames. But gather these straws into a bundle and light them, and you get a mighty fire, rising like a column into the sky; public prayer is like that."

SIXTUS II, pope and martyr, and COMPANIONS, martyrs
(d.258)

Freedom to assemble has always been one of the first liberties that dictators deny to subjects (and one highly prized by our American forefathers). The emperor Valerian published his first decree against Christians in 257, and forbade them to hold assemblies. Pope Sixtus had been pope for just one year when he was murdered while presiding at the Eucharist in one of the underground caverns used as cemeteries (catacombs). He and four deacons were seized and beheaded. Two other deacons were probably martyred the same day, and St. Lawrence (August 10) four days later.

During his year in office Sixtus had to deal with the controversy about the validity of baptism by heretics. He supported the positive view, but was tolerant toward the practice of the Eastern Church, which rebaptized those who had received the sacrament from heretics. The negative view was shared by St. Cyprian (Sept. 16) to whom Sixtus sent messengers for discussion. Sixtus was asked to be patient with those in error, and contented himself with a strong recommendation of the truth. Other popes did the same, until the error was finally condemned.

COMMENT: What are we willing to suffer to practice our faith? In times of persecution Christians have always dared to come together to celebrate the

Eucharist — huddled in a corner of the prison, risking life and possessions — in Ireland, for example,
by providing "priest's holes." Those of us who live in
Christian lands can scarcely comprehend the
possibility: does the Eucharist mean so much to us
that, under government persecution, we would
gather at night in one of our homes to celebrate the
mystery of the body and blood of Jesus, risking that
fatal knock on the door?

QUOTE: Baptism, of itself, is only a beginning, a
point of departure, for it is wholly directed toward
the acquiring of fullness of life in Christ. Baptism is
thus oriented toward a complete profession of faith,
a complete incorporation into the system of salvation such as Christ himself willed it to be, and
finally, toward a complete participation in
Eucharistic communion (Vatican II, Ecumenism,
22).

August 7   *Optional*

CAJETAN, priest
(1480-1547)

Like most of us, Cajetan seemed headed for an
"ordinary" life — first as a lawyer, then as a priest
engaged in the work of the Roman curia.

His life took a characteristic turn when he joined
the Oratory of Divine Love in Rome, a group
devoted to piety and charity, shortly after his ordination at 36. When he was 42 he founded a hospital for incurables at Venice. At Vicenza, he entered

a "disreputable" religious community that consisted only of men of the lowest stations of life — and was roundly censured by his friends, who thought his action was a reflection on his family. He sought out the sick and poor of the town and served them.

The greatest need of the time was the reformation of a Church that was "sick in head and members." Cajetan and three friends decided that the best road to reformation lay in reviving the spirit and zeal of the clergy. Together (one of them later became Paul IV) they founded a congregation known as the Theatines (from Teate (Chieti) where their first superior-bishop had his see). They managed to escape to Venice after their house in Rome was wrecked when Charles V sacked Rome in 1527. The Theatines were outstanding among the Catholic reform movements that took shape before the Protestant reformation.

He founded a *monte de pieta* (mountain [or fund] of piety) in Naples — one of many charitable, non-profit credit organizations that lent money on the security of pawned objects. The purpose was to help the poor and protect them against usurers. Cajetan's little organization ultimately became the Bank of Naples, with great changes in policy.

STORY: When Cajetan was sent to establish a house of his congregation in Naples, a count tried to prevail upon him to accept an estate in lands. He refused. The count pointed out that he would need the money, for the people of Naples were not as generous as the people of Venice. "That may be true, replied Cajetan, but God is the same in both cities."

COMMENT: If Vatican II had been summarily stopped after its first session in 1962, many Catholics would have felt that a great blow had been dealt to the growth of the Church. Cajetan had the same feeling about the Council of Trent. But, as he said, God is the same in Naples as in Venice, with or without Trent or Vatican II (or III). We open ourselves to God's power in whatever circumstances we find ourselves, and God's will is done. He has standards of success that are different from ours.

August 8   *Memorial*

DOMINIC, priest
(1170-1221)

If he hadn't taken a trip with his bishop, Dominic would probably have remained within the structure of contemplative life; after the trip, he spent the rest of his life being a contemplative in active apostolic work.

Born in old Castile, Spain, he was trained for the priesthood by a priest-uncle, studied the arts and theology, and became a canon of the cathedral at Osma, where there was an attempt to revive the apostolic common life of the Acts of the Apostles.

On a journey to northern Europe with his bishop, he came face to face with the then virulent Albigensian heresy at Languedoc. The Albigensians (Cathari, "the pure") held to two principles, one good, one evil, in the world. All matter is evil — hence they denied the Incarnation and sacraments.

42

On the same principle they abstained from procreation and took a minimum of food and drink. The inner circle led what must be called a heroic life of purity and asceticism not shared by ordinary followers.

Dominic sensed the need of the Church to combat the heresy, and was commissioned to be part of the preaching crusade against it. He saw immediately why the preaching was not succeeding: the ordinary people admired and followed the ascetical heroes of the Albigenses. Understandably they were not impressed by the Catholic spokesmen who traveled with horses and retinues, stayed at the best inns, and had servants. Dominic therefore, with three Cistercians, began itinerant preaching according to the Gospel ideal. He continued this work for 10 years, being successful with the ordinary people but not with the leaders.

His fellow preachers gradually became a community, and in 1215 he founded a religious house at Toulouse which was to be the beginning of the Dominican Order.

His ideal, and that of his Order, was to link organically a life with God, study, prayer in all forms, with a ministry of salvation to men by the word of God. His ideal: *contemplata tradere:* "to pass on the fruits of contemplation" or "to speak only of God or with God."

COMMENT: The Dominican ideal, like that of all religious communities, is for the imitation, not merely the admiration, of the rest of the Church. The effective combining of contemplation and activity is the vocation of truck driver John Smith as well as Theologian Thomas Aquinas. Acquired contemplation is the tranquil abiding in the presence of God, and is an integral part of any full human life. It must be the wellspring of all Christian activity.

STORY: Legend has it that Dominic saw the sinful world threatened by God's anger but saved by the intercession of our Lady, who pointed out to her Son two figures: one was Dominic himself, the other a stranger. In church the next day he saw a ragged beggar enter — the man in the vision. He went up to him, embraced him and said, "You are my companion and must walk with me. If we hold together, no earthly power can withstand us." The beggar was Francis of Assisi. The meeting of the two founders is commemorated twice a year, when on their respective feast-days Dominicans and Franciscans celebrate Mass in each other's churches, and afterwards sit at the same table "to eat the bread which for seven centuries has never been wanting" *(Butler's Lives of the Saints).*

August 10   *Feast*

LAWRENCE, deacon and martyr
(d. 258?)

The esteem in which the Church holds Lawrence is seen in the fact that today's celebration ranks as a feast. We know very little about his life. He is one of those whose martyrdom made a deep and lasting impression on the early Church. Celebration of his feast day spread rapidly.

He was a Roman deacon under Pope St. Sixtus II (Aug. 5). Four days after this pope was put to death, Lawrence and four clerics suffered martyrdom, probably during the persecution of the Emperor Valerian.

Legendary details of his death were known to Damasus, Prudentius, Ambrose and Augustine. The church built over his tomb became one of the seven principal churches in Rome and a favorite place for Roman pilgrimages.

COMMENT: Once again we have a saint about whom almost nothing is known, yet one who has received extraordinary honor in the Church since the 4th century. Almost nothing — yet the greatest fact of his life is certain: he died for Christ. We who are hungry for details about the lives of the saints are again reminded that their holiness was, after all, total response to Christ, expressed perfectly by a death like his.

STORY: A well-known legend has persisted from earliest times. As deacon in Rome, Lawrence was charged with the responsibility for the material goods of the Church, and the distribution of alms to the poor. When Lawrence knew he would be arrested like the Pope, he sought out the poor, widows and orphans of Rome and gave them all the money he had on hand, selling even the sacred vessels to increase the sum. When the prefect of Rome heard of this, he imagined that the Christians must have considerable treasure. He sent for Lawrence and said, "You Christians say we are cruel to you, but that is not what I have in mind. I am told that your priests offer in gold, that the sacred blood is received in silver cups, that you have golden candlesticks at your evening services. Now, your doctrine says you must render to Caesar what is his. Bring these treasures — the emperor needs them to maintain his forces. God does not cause money to be coined: he brought none of it into the world with him — only words. Give me the money, therefore, and be rich in words."

Lawrence replied that the Church was indeed rich. "I will show you a valuable part. But give me time to set everything in order and make an inventory." After three days he gathered a great number of the blind, lame, maimed, lepers, orphans and widows and put them in rows. When the prefect arrived, Lawrence simply said, "These are the treasure of the Church."

The prefect was so angry he told Lawrence that he would indeed have his wish to die — but it would be by inches. He had a great gridiron prepared, with coals beneath it, and had Lawrence's body placed on it. After the martyr had suffered the pain for a long time, the legend concludes, he made his famous cheerful remark, "It is well done. Turn it over and eat it!"

CLARE, virgin
(1194-1253)

One of the more sugary movies made about Francis of Assisi pictures Clare as a golden-haired beauty floating through sun-drenched fields, a sort of one-girl counterpart to the new Franciscan Order.

The beginning of her religious life was indeed movie material. Having refused to marry at 15, she was moved by the dynamic preaching of Francis. He became her lifelong friend and spiritual guide.

At 18, she escaped one night from her father's home, was met on the road to the Portiuncula by friars carrying torches, and in that poor little chapel received a rough woolen habit, exchanged her

jeweled belt for a common rope with knots in it, and sacrificed the long tresses to Francis' scissors. He placed her in a Benedictine convent which her father and uncles immediately stormed in rage. She clung to the altar of the church, threw aside her veil to show her cropped hair, and remained adamant.

End of movie material. Sixteen days later her sister Agnes joined her. Others came. They lived a simple life of great poverty, austerity and complete seclusion from the world, according to a rule Francis gave them as the Second Order (Poor Clares). At

21, Francis obliged her under obedience to accept the office of abbess, in which she continued until her death.

The nuns went barefoot, slept on the ground, ate no meat, and observed almost complete silence. (Later Clare, like Francis, persuaded her sisters to moderate this rigor: "Our bodies are not made of brass.") The greatest emphasis, of course was on Gospel poverty. They possessed no property, even in common, subsisting on daily contributions. When even the Pope tried to persuade her to mitigate this practice, she showed her characteristic firmness: "I need to be absolved from my sins, but I do not wish to be absolved from the obligation of following Jesus Christ."

Contemporary accounts glow with admiration of her life in the convent of San Damiano in Assisi. She served the sick, waited on table, washed the feet of the begging nuns. She came from prayer, it was said, with her face so shining it dazzled those about her. She suffered serious illness for the last 27 years of her life. Her influence was such that popes, cardinals and bishops often came to consult her — she herself never left the walls of San Damiano.

Francis always remained her great friend and inspiration. She was always obedient to his will, and to the great ideal of Gospel life which he was making real.

A well-known story concerns her prayer and trust. She had the Blessed Sacrament placed on the walls of the convent when it faced attack by invading Saracens. "Does it please you, O God, to deliver into the hands of these beasts the defenseless children I have nourished with your love? I beseech you, dear Lord, protect these whom I am now unable to protect." To her sisters she said, "Don't be afraid. Trust in Jesus." The Saracens fled.

COMMENT: The 41 years of Clare's religious life are poor movie material, but they are a scenario of sanctity: an indomitable resolve to lead the simple, literal Gospel life as Francis taught her; courageous resistance to the ever-present pressure to dilute the ideal; a passion for poverty and humility; an ardent life of prayer, and a generous concern for her sisters.

STORY: On her deathbed, Clare was heard to say to herself: "Go forth in peace, for you have followed the good road. Go forth without fear, for he who created you has made you holy, has always protected you, and loves you as a mother. Blessed be you, my God, for having created me."

August 13   *Optional*

PONTIAN, pope and martyr, HIPPOLYTUS, priest and martyr
(d.235)

Two men died for the faith after harsh treatment and exhaustion in the mines of Sardinia. One had been pope for five years, the other an anti-pope for 18. They died reconciled.

Pontian

Pontian was a Roman who served as pope from

230 to 235. During his reign he held a synod which confirmed the excommunication of the great theologian Origen in Alexandria. He was banished to exile by the Roman emperor in 235, and resigned so that a successor could be elected in Rome. He was sent to the "unhealthy" island of Sardinia, where he died of harsh treatment in 235. With him was Hippolytus, (see below) with whom he was reconciled. The bodies of both martyrs were brought back to Rome and buried with solemn rites as martyrs.

Hippolytus

As a presbyter in Rome, Hippolytus (the name means "a horse turned loose") was at first "holier than the Church." He censured the Pope for not coming down hard enough on a certain heresy — calling him a tool in the hands of one Callistus, a deacon — and coming close to advocating the opposite heresy himself. When Callistus was elected pope, Hippolytus accused him of being too lenient with penitents, and had himself elected antipope by a group of followers. He felt that the Church must be composed of pure souls uncompromisingly separated from the world, and evidently thought that his group fitted the description. He remained in schism through the reigns of three popes. In 235 he was also banished to the island of Sardinia. Shortly before or after this event, he was reconciled to the Church, and died with Pope Pontian in exile.

Hippolytus was a rigorist, a vehement and intransigent man for whom even orthodox doctrine and practice was not purified enough. He is, nevertheless, the most important theologian and prolific religious writer before the age of Constantine. His writings are the fullest source of our knowledge of the Roman liturgy and the structure of the Church in the second and third centuries. His works include many scripture commentaries, polemics against heresies, and a history of the world. In 1551 a marble statue, dating from the third century, was found, representing the saint sitting in a chair. On one side is inscribed his table for computing the date of Easter, on the other a list of how it works until the year 224. Pope John XXIII installed the statue in the Vatican library.

COMMENT: Hippolytus was a strong defender of orthodoxy, and admitted his excesses by his humble reconciliation. He was not a formal heretic, but an over-zealous disciplinarian. What he could not learn in his prime as a reformer and purist, he learned in the pain and desolation of imprisonment. It was a fitting symbolic event that Pope Pontian shared his martyrdom.

QUOTE: "Christ, like a skillful physician, understands the weakness of men. He loves to teach the ignorant and the erring he turns again to his own true way. He is easily found by those who live by faith; and to those of pure eye and holy heart, who desire to knock at the door, he opens immediately. He does not disdain the barbarian, nor does he set the eunuch aside as no man. He does not hate the female on account of the woman's act of disobedience in the beginning, nor does he reject the male on account of the man's transgression. But he seeks all, and desires to save all, wishing to make all the children of God,

and calling all the saints unto one perfect man"
(Hippolytus, *Treatise on Christ and Antichrist*).

STEPHEN OF HUNGARY
(975-1038)

The Church is universal, but its expression is always affected—for good or ill—by local culture.
There are no "pure" Christians; there are Mexican
Christians, Polish Christians, Filipino Christians,
etc. This fact is evident in the life of Stephen, national hero and spiritual patron of Hungary.

Born a pagan, he was baptized about the age of
10, together with his father, chief of the Magyars, a
fierce group of marauders who came to the Danube
in the ninth century. At 20, he married Gisela, sister
of the future Emperor St. Henry (July 13). When he
succeeded his father, Stephen adopted a policy of
Christianization of the country for both political and
religious reasons. He suppressed a series of revolts
by pagan nobles and welded the Magyars into a
strong national group. He sent to Rome to get ecclesiastical organization—and also to ask the Pope
to confer the title of king upon him. He was crowned
on Christmas day in 1001.

Stephen established a system of tithes to support
churches and pastors and to relieve the poor. Out of
every 10 towns one had to build a church and support a priest. He abolished pagan customs with a certain amount of violence, and commanded all to marry, except clergy and religious. He was easily ac-

cessible to all, especially the poor.

In 1031 his son Emeric died, and the rest of his days were embittered by controversy over his successor. His nephews attempted to kill him. He died in 1038 and was canonized, along with his son, in 1083.

COMMENT: God's gift of holiness is a Christlike love of God and man. Love must sometimes bear a stern countenance, for the sake of ultimate good. Christ attacked the hypocrisy of the Pharisees, but died forgiving them. Paul excommunicated the incestuous man at Corinth "that his spirit may be saved." Some Christians fought the Crusades with noble zeal, in spite of the unworthy motives of others. Today, after senseless wars, and with a deeper understanding of the complex nature of human motives, we shrink from any use of violence, physical or "silent." This is a wholesome development, but it does not seem possible for a Christian to be an absolute pacifist. Sometimes evil must be repelled by force.

QUOTE: "Although the Church has contributed much to the development of culture, experience shows that, because of circumstances, it is sometimes difficult to harmonize culture with Christian teaching. These difficulties do not necessarily harm the life of faith. Indeed they can stimulate the mind to a more accurate and penetrating grasp of the faith. For recent studies and findings in science, history and philosophy raise new questions which influence life and demand new theological investigations" (Vatican II, The Church Today, 62).

JOHN EUDES, priest
(1601-1680)

How little we know where God's grace will lead. Born on a farm in northern France, John died in the next "county" or department 79 years later. In that time he was a religious, a parish missionary, the founder of two religious communities, and one of the greatest promoters of the devotion to the Sacred Heart and the Heart of Mary.

He joined the religious community of the Oratorians and was ordained priest at 24. During severe plagues in 1627 and 1631 he volunteered to care for the stricken in his own diocese. Lest he infect his fellow religious, he lived in a huge cask in the middle of a field during the plague.

At age 32, John became a parish missionary. His gifts as preacher and confessor won him great popularity. He preached over 100 parish missions, some lasting from several weeks to several months.

In his concern with the spiritual improvement of the clergy, he realized that the greatest need was for seminaries. He had permission from his general superior, the bishop and even Cardinal Richelieu to begin this work; but the succeeding general superior disapproved. After prayer and counsel, John decided it was best to leave the religious community. The same year he founded a new one, ultimately called the Eudists (Congregation of Jesus and Mary), devoted to the formation of the clergy by conducting diocesan seminaries. The new venture, while approved by individual bishops, met with immediate opposition, especially from Jansenists and some of his former associates. John founded several seminaries in Normandy, but was unable to get approval from Rome (partly, it was said, because he did not use the most tactful approach).

In his parish mission work John was disturbed by the sad condition of prostitutes who sought to escape their miserable life. Temporary shelters were found, but arrangements were not satisfactory. A certain Madeleine Lamy, who had cared for several of the women, one day said to him, "Where are you off to now? To some church, I suppose, where you'll gaze at the images and think yourself pious. And all the time what is really wanted of you is a decent house for these poor creatures." The words, and the laughter of those present, stuck deep within him. The result was another new religious community, called the Sisters of Charity of the Refuge.

He is probably best known for the central theme of his writings: Jesus as the source of holiness, Mary as the model of the Christian life. His devotion to the Sacred Heart, and to the Heart of Mary, led Pius XI to declare him the father of the liturgical cultus of the Hearts of Jesus and Mary.

COMMENT: Holiness is the wholehearted openness to the love of God. It is visibly expressed in many ways, but the variety of expression has one common quality: concern for the needs of others. In John's case, those who were in need were plague stricken people, ordinary parishioners, those preparing for the priesthood, prostitutes, and all Christians called to imitate the love of Jesus and his mother.

QUOTE: "Our wish, our object, our chief preoccupation must be to form Jesus in ourselves, to make his spirit, his devotion, his affections, his desires and his disposition live and reign there. All our religious exercises should be directed to this end. It is the work which God has given us to do unceasingly" (St. John Eudes, *The Life and Reign of Jesus in Christian Souls"*).

August 20   *Memorial*

BERNARD, abbot and doctor
(1091-1153)

Man of the century! You see it applied to so many today — "Golfer of the century," "Composer of the century," "Right tackle of the century" that the line no longer has any punch. But "Man of the 12th century!" There is no doubt or controversy. It has to be Bernard of Clairvaux. Adviser of popes, preacher of the Second Crusade, defender of the faith, healer of a schism, reformer of a monastic order, Scripture scholar, theologian and eloquent preacher. Any one title would distinguish an ordinary man. Yet Bernard was all of these, and he still retained a burning desire to return to the hidden monastic life of his younger days.

In the year 1111, at the age of 16, Bernard left his home to join the monastic community of Citeaux. His five brothers, two uncles and some 30 young friends followed him into the monastery. Within four years a dying community had recovered enough vitality to establish a new house in the nearby valley

57

of "Wormwood," with Bernard as abbot. The zealous young man was quite demanding, though more on himself than others. A slight breakdown of health taught him to be more patient and understanding. The valley was soon renamed Clairvaux, the valley of light.

His ability as arbitrator and counselor became widely known. More and more he was lured away from the monastery to settle long-standing disputes. On several of these occasions he apparently stepped on some sensitive toes in Rome. Bernard was completely dedicated to the primacy of the Roman See. But to a letter of warning from Rome he replied that the good fathers in Rome had enough to do to keep the Church in one piece. If any matters arose that warranted their interest, he would be the first to let them know.

Shortly thereafter it was Bernard who intervened in a full-blown schism and settled it in favor of the Roman Pontiff against the antipope.

The Holy See prevailed on Bernard to preach the Second Crusade throughout Europe. His eloquence was so overwhelming that a great army was assembled and the success of the crusade seemed assured. The ideals of the men and their leaders, however, were not those of Abbot Bernard, and the project ended as a complete military and moral disaster.

Bernard felt responsible in some way for the degenerative effects of the crusade. This heavy burden possibly hastened his death, which came August 20, 1153.

COMMENT: Bernard's life in the Church was more active than we can imagine possible today. His efforts produced far-reaching results. But he knew that they would have availed little without the many hours of prayer and contemplation that brought him strength and heavenly direction. His life was characterized by a deep devotion to the Blessed Mother. His sermons and books about Mary are still the standard of Marian theology.

QUOTE: "In dangers, in doubts, in difficulties, think of Mary, call upon Mary. Let not her name depart from your lips, never suffer it to leave your heart. And that you may more surely obtain the assistance of her prayer, neglect not to walk in her footsteps. With her for guide, you shall never go astray; while invoking her, you shall never lose heart; so long as she is in your mind, you are safe from deception; while she holds your hand, you cannot fall; under her protection you have nothing to fear; if she walks before you, you shall not grow weary; if she shows you favor, you shall reach the goal" (St. Bernard).

August 21   *Memorial*

PIUS X, pope
(1835-1914)

Pope Pius X is perhaps best remembered for his encouragement of the frequent reception of Holy Communion, especially by children.

The second of 10 children in a poor Italian family, Joseph Sarto, at 68, became Pius X, one of the 20th century's greatest popes.

Ever mindful of his humble origin, he stated, "I was born poor, I lived poor, I will die poor." He was embarrassed by some of the pomp of the papal court. "Look how they have dressed me up," he said in tears to an old friend. To another, "It is a penance to be forced to accept all these practices. They lead me around surrounded by soldiers like Jesus when he was seized in Gethsemane."

Interested in politics, he encouraged Italian Catholics to become more politically involved. One of his first papal acts was to end the supposed right of governments to interfere by veto in papal elections — a practice that threatened the freedom of the conclave in which he was elected.

In 1905 when France renounced its agreement with the Holy See and threatened confiscation of Church property if governmental control of Church affairs were not granted, Pius X courageously rejected the demand.

While he did not author a famous social encyclical like his predecessor, he denounced the ill treatment of the Indians on the plantations of Peru, sent a relief commission to Messina after an earthquake, and sheltered refugees at his own expense.

On the 11th anniversary of his election as pope, Europe was plunged into World War I. He had foreseen it, but it killed him. "This is the last affliction the Lord will visit on me. I would gladly give my life to save my poor children from this ghastly scourge." He died a few weeks after the war began.

COMMENT: His humble background was no obstacle in relating to a personal God and to people whom he loved genuinely. He gained his strength, his gentleness and warmth for people from the source of all gifts, the Spirit of Jesus. In contrast, we often feel embarrassed by our simple backgrounds. Shame makes us prefer to remain aloof from people whom we perceive as superior. If we are in a superior position, on the other hand, we often ignore simple people. Yet, we, too, have to help "restore all things in Christ," especially the wounded people of God.

QUOTE: Describing Pius X, a historian wrote that he was "a man of God who knew the unhappiness of the world and the hardships of life, and in the greatness of his heart wanted to comfort everyone."

August 23   *Optional*

ROSE OF LIMA, virgin
(1586-1617)

The first canonized saint of the New World has one characteristic of all saints: the suffering of opposition; and another characteristic which is rather for admiration than imitation: excessive practices of mortification.

She was born to parents of Spanish descent in Lima, Peru, at a time when South America was in its first century of evangelization. She seems to have taken Catherine of Siena as a model, in spite of the objections and ridicule of parents and friends.

The saints have so great a love of God that what seems "kooky" to us, and is indeed sometimes imprudent, is simply a logical carrying out of a conviction that *anything* that might endanger a loving relationship with God must be rooted out. So, because her beauty was so often admired, Rose used to rub her face with pepper to produce disfiguring blotches. Later, she wore a thick circlet of silver on her head, studded on the inside, like a crown of thorns.

When her parents fell into financial trouble, she worked in the garden all day and sewed at night. Ten years of struggle against her parents began when they tried to make Rose marry. They refused to let her enter a convent, and out of obedience she continued her life of penance and solitude at home, as a member of the Third Order of St. Dominic. So deep was her desire to live the life of Christ that she spent most of her time at home in solitude.

During the last few years of her life, Rose set up a room in the house, where she cared for homeless children, the elderly and the sick. This was a beginning of social services in Peru. Though secluded in life and activity, she was brought to the attention of Inquisition interrogators, who could only say that she was influenced by grace.

What might have been a merely eccentric life was transfigured from the inside, and if we remember some unusual penances, we should also remember the greatest thing about her: a love of God so ardent that it withstood ridicule from without, violent temptation and lengthy periods of sickness. When she died at 31, the city turned out for her funeral. Prominent men took turns carrying her coffin.

COMMENT: It is easy to dismiss "excessive" penances of the saints as the expression of a certain culture or temperament. But a woman wearing a crown of thorns may at least prod our consciences. For all our inflation and energy crisis, we enjoy the most comfort-oriented life in the history of man. We eat too much, drink too much, use a million gadgets, fill our eyes and ears with everything imaginable. Commerce thrives on creating useless needs to spend our money on. It seems that when we have become most like slaves, there is the greatest talk of "freedom." Are we willing to discipline ourselves in such an atmosphere?

QUOTE: "If your hand or your foot is your undoing, cut it off and throw it from you. Better to enter life maimed or crippled than be thrown with two hands or two feet into endless fire. If your eye is your downfall, gouge it out and cast it from you! Better to enter life with one eye than be thrown with both in fiery Gehenna" (Matt. 18,8-9).

August 24   *Feast*

BARTHOLOMEW, apostle

In the New Testament, Bartholomew is mentioned only in the lists of the apostles. Some scholars identify him with Nathaniel, a man of Cana in Galilee who was summoned to Jesus by Philip. Jesus paid him a great compliment: "This man is a true Israelite. There is no guile in him." When Nathanael asked how Jesus knew him, Jesus said, "I saw you under the fig tree." Whatever amazing revelation this involved, it brought Nathanael to exclaim, "You

63

are the Son of God; you are the king of Israel." But Jesus countered with, "Do you believe just because I told you that I saw you under the fig tree? You will see much greater things than that!"

Nathanael did see greater things. He was one of those to whom Jesus appeared on the shore of the Sea of Galilee after his resurrection. They had been fishing all night without success. In the morning, they saw someone standing on the shore though no one knew it was Jesus. He told them to cast their net again, and they made so great a catch that they could not haul the net in. Then John cried out to Peter, "It is the Lord!"

When they brought the boat to shore, they found a fire burning, with some fish laid on it and some bread. Jesus asked them to bring some of the fish they had caught, and invited them to come and eat their meal. John relates that although they knew it was Jesus, none of the apostles presumed to inquire who he was. This, John notes, was the third time Jesus appeared to the apostles.

COMMENT: Bartholomew or Nathanael—in any case we are confronted again with the fact that we know almost nothing about most of the apostles. Yet the unknown ones were also foundation stones, the 12 pillars of the new Israel, whose 12 tribes now encompass the whole earth. Their personalities were secondary, without thereby being demeaned, to their great office of bearing tradition from their first-hand experience, speaking in the name of Jesus, putting the Word made flesh into human words for the enlightenment of the world. Their holiness was not an introverted contemplation of their status before God. It was a gift that they had to share with others. The Good News was that all men are called to the holiness of being Christ's members, by the gracious gift of God.

The simple fact is that man is totally meaningless unless God is his total concern. Then his humanity, made holy with the holiness of God himself, becomes the most precious creation of God.

QUOTE: "Like Christ himself, the Apostles were unceasingly bent on bearing witness to the truth of God. They showed special courage in speaking 'the word of God with boldness' before the people and their rulers. With a firm faith they held that the Gospel is indeed the power of God unto salvation for all who believe. They followed the example of gentleness and respectfulness of Christ" (Vatican II, Religious Freedom, 11).

August 25   *Optional*

LOUIS
(1226-1270)

At his coronation as King of France, Louis bound himself by oath to behave as God's anointed, as the father of his people and feudal lord of the King of Peace. Other kings had done the same, of course. Louis was different in that he actually interpreted his kingly duties in the light of faith. After the violence of two previous reigns, he brought peace and justice.

He was crowned king at 12, at his father's death. His mother, Blanche of Castile, ruled during his minority. When he was 19, (and his bride 12) he was married to Marguerite of Provence. It was a loving marriage, despite her arrogant and restless nature. They had 10 children.

Louis "took the cross" for a crusade when he was 30. His army took Damietta on the Nile but not long after, weakened by dysentery and without support, they were surrounded and captured. Louis obtained the release of the army by giving up the city of Damietta in addition to paying a ransom. He stayed in Syria four years.

He is admired as a crusader, but perhaps greater credit is due him for his concern for justice in civil administration. He drew up regulations for his officials became the first of a series of reform laws. He replaced trial by battle with a form of examination of witnesses, and encouraged the beginning of the use of written records in court.

Louis was always respectful of the papacy, but defended royal interests against the popes, and refused to acknowledge Innocent IV's sentence against the emperor Frederick II.

He was devoted to his people, founding hospitals, visiting the sick, like his patron St. Francis caring even for lepers, (he is one of the patrons of the Third Order of St. Francis). Louis united France— lords and townsfolk, peasants and priests and knights—by the force of his personality and holiness. For many years the nation was at peace.

Disturbed by new Moslem advances in Syria, he led a second crusade in 1267, at the age of 41. His crusade was diverted to Tunis for his brother's sake. The army was decimated by disease within a month, and Louis himself died on foreign soil at the age of 44. He was canonized 27 years later.

COMMENT: Louis was strong-willed, strong-minded. His word was utterly trusted, and his courage in action was remarkable. What is most remarkable was his sense of respect for anyone with whom he dealt, especially the "humble folk of the Lord." To care for his people, he built cathedrals, churches, libraries, hospitals and orphanages. He dealt with princes honestly and equitably. He hoped to be treated the same way by the King of Kings, to whom he gave his life, his family and his country.

STORY: Every day Louis had 13 special guests from among the poor to eat with him, and a large number of poor were served meals near his palace. During Advent and Lent all who presented themselves were given a meal, and Louis often served them in person. He kept lists of needy people, whom he regularly relieved, in every province of his dominion.

August 25   *Optional*

JOSEPH CALASANZ, priest
(1556-1648)

From Aragon, where he was born in 1556, to Rome, where he died 92 years later, fortune alternately smiled and frowned on the work of Joseph Calasanz. A priest with university training in canon law and theology, respected for his wisdom and administrative expertise, he put aside his career because he was deeply concerned with the need for education of poor children. When he was unable to get other institutes to undertake this apostolate at Rome, he and several companions personally provided a free school for deprived children. So overwhelming was the response that there was a constant need for larger facilities to house their effort. Soon Pope Clement VIII gave support to the school, and this aid continued under Pope Paul V. Other schools were opened; other men were attracted to the work, and in 1621 the community (for so the teachers lived) was recognized as a religious community, the Clerks Regular of Religious Schools or the Piarists (Scolopi). Not long after, Joseph was appointed superior for life.

A combination of various prejudices and political ambition and manuevering was to cause the institute much turmoil. There were those who did not favor educating the poor, for education would leave the poor dissatisfied with their lowly tasks for society! Others were shocked that some of the Piarists were sent for instruction to Galileo (a friend of Joseph) as superior, thus dividing the members into opposite camps. Repeatedly investigated by papal commissions, Joseph was demoted; when the struggle within the institute persisted, the Piarists were suppressed. Only after Joseph's death were they restored to status as a religious community.

COMMENT: No one knew better than Joseph the need for the work he was doing; no one knew better than he how baseless were the charges brought against him. Yet if he was to work within the Church, he realized that he must submit to its authority, that he must accept a setback if he was unable to convince authorized investigators. While the prejudice, the scheming, and the ignorance of men often keep the truth from emerging for a long period of time, Joseph was convinced, even under suppression, that his institute would again be recognized and authorized. With this trust he joined exceptional patience and a genuine spirit of forgiveness.

QUOTE: Even in the days after his own demotion, Joseph protected his persecutors against his enroused partisans; and when the community was suppressed, he stated with Job, to whom he was often compared: "The Lord gave and the Lord has taken away. Blessed be the name of the Lord."

MONICA
(322?-387)

The circumstances of St. Monica's life could have made her a nagging wife, a bitter daughter-in-law and a despairing parent, yet she did not give way to any of these temptations. Although she was a Christian, her parents gave her in marriage to a pagan, Patricius, who lived in her home town of Tagaste in North Africa. Patricius had some redeeming features, but he had a violent temper and was licentious. Monica also had to bear with a cantankerous mother-in-law who lived in her home.

Patricius criticized his wife because of her charity and piety, but always respected her. Monica's prayers and example finally won her husband and mother-in-law to Christianity. Her husband died in 371, one year after his baptism.

Monica had at least three children who survived infancy. The oldest, Augustine, is the most famous. At the time of his father's death, Augustine was 17 and a rhetoric student in Carthage. Monica was distressed to learn that her son had accepted the Manichean heresy and was living an immoral life. For a while, she refused to let him eat or sleep in her house. Then one night she had a vision that assured her Augustine would return to the faith. From that time on she stayed close to her son, praying and fasting for him. In fact, she often stayed much closer than Augustine wanted.

When he was 29, Augustine decided to go to Rome to teach rhetoric. She was determined to go along. One night he told his mother that he was going to the dock to say "good-bye" to a friend. Instead, he set sail for Rome. Monica was heartbroken when she learned of Augustine's trick, but she still followed him. She arrived in Rome only to find that he had left for Milan. Although travel was difficult, Monica pursued him to Milan.

In Milan Augustine came under the influence of the bishop, St. Ambrose, who also became Monica's spiritual director. She accepted his advice in everything and had the humility to give up some practices that had become second nature to her. (See quote.) Monica became a leader of the devout women in Milan as she had been in Tagaste.

She continued her prayers for Augustine during his years of instruction. At Easter, 387, St. Ambrose baptized Augustine and several of his friends. Soon after, his party left for Africa. Although no one else was aware of it, Monica knew her life was near the end. She told Augustine, "Son, nothing in this world now affords me delight. I do not know what there is now left for me to do or why I am still here, all my hopes in this world being now fulfilled." She became ill shortly after and suffered severely for nine days before her death.

Almost all we know about St. Monica is in the writings of St. Augustine, especially his *Confessions.*

COMMENT: Today, with our instant cereal, instant cures and instant credit, we have little patience for things that take time. Likewise, we want instant answers to our prayers. Monica is a model of patience. Her long years of prayer, coupled with a strong, well-disciplined character finally led to the conversion of her hot-tempered husband, her cantankerous mother-in-law and her brilliant but wayward son, Augustine.

QUOTE: When Monica moved from North Africa to Milan, she found religious practices new to her and also that some of her former customs, such as a Saturday fast, were not common there. She asked St. Ambrose which customs she should follow. His classic reply was: "When I am here, I do not fast on Saturday, but I fast when I am in Rome; do the same and always follow the custom and discipline of the Church as it is observed in the particular locality in which you find yourself."

AUGUSTINE, bishop and doctor
(354-430)

A Christian at 33, a priest at 36, a bishop at 41. Everyone is familiar with the sketch-biography of Augustine of Hippo, sinner turned saint. But to really get to know the man is a rewarding experience.

There quickly surfaces the intensity with which he lived his life, whether his path lead away from, or toward God. The tears of his mother, the instructions of Ambrose, and, most of all, God himself speaking to him in the Scriptures redirected Augustine's love of life to a life of love ("Too late have I loved you, O Beauty so ancient and so new!")

Having been so deeply immersed in creature-pride of life in his early days and having drunk deeply of its bitter dregs, it is not surprising that Augustine should have turned, with a holy fierceness, against the many demon-thrusts rampant in his day. His times were truly decadent—politically, socially, morally. He was both feared and loved, like the Master. The perennial criticism: a fundamental rigorism.

In his day, he providentially fulfilled the office of prophet. Like Jeremiah and other greats, he was hard pressed but could not keep quiet. "I say to myself, I will not mention him, I will speak in his name no more. But then it becomes like fire burning in my heart, imprisoned in my bones; I grow weary holding it in, I cannot endure it" (Is. 20,9).

COMMENT: Augustine is still acclaimed and condemned in our day. (Cf. *Whatever Became of Sin?* by Karl Menninger.) He is a prophet for today, trumpeting the need to scrap escapisms and stand face to face with personal responsibility and dignity.

QUOTE: "Too late have I loved you, O Beauty of ancient days, yet ever new! Too late I loved you! And behold, you were within, and I abroad, and there I searched for you; I was deformed, plunging amid those fair forms, which you had made. You were with me, but I was not with you. Things held me far from you—things which, if they were not in you, were not at all. You called, and shouted, and burst my deafness. You flashed and shone, and scattered my blindness. You breathed odors and I drew in breath—and I pant for you. I tasted, and I hunger and thirst. You touched me, and I burned for your peace" (St. Augustine, *Confessions,* book 10, ch. 27).

BEHEADING OF
JOHN THE BAPTIST,
martyr

The drunken oath of a king with a shallow sense of honor, a seductive dance, and the hateful heart of a queen, joined together to bring about the martyrdom of John the Baptist. The greatest of prophets suffered the fate of so many Old Testament prophets before him: rejection and martyrdom. The "voice crying in the desert" did not hesitate to accuse the guilty, did not hesitate to speak the truth. But why? What possesses a man that he would give us his very life?

This great religious reformer was sent by God to prepare the people for the Messiah. His vocation was one of selfless giving. The only power that he claimed was the Spirit of Yahweh. "I baptize you in water for the sake of reform, but the one who will follow me is more powerful than I. I am not even fit to carry his sandals. It is he who will baptize you in the Holy Spirit and fire" (Matt. 3,11). Scripture tells us that many people followed John, looking to him for hope, perhaps in anticipation of some great Messianic power. John never allowed himself the false honor of receiving these people for his own glory. He knew his calling was one of preparation. When the time came, he led his disciples to Jesus. "The next day John was there again with two of his disciples. As he watched Jesus walk by he said, 'Look! There is the Lamb of God!' The two disciples heard what he said, and followed Jesus" (John 1,35-37).

It is John the Baptist who has pointed the way to Christ. His life and death were a giving-over of self for God and man. His simple style of life was one of complete detachment from earthly possessions. His heart was centered on God and the call that he heard from the Spirit of God speaking to his heart. Confident of God's grace, he had the courage to speak words of condemnation, of repentance, of salvation.

COMMENT: Each person has a calling to which he must listen. No one will ever repeat the mission of

John, and yet all of us are called to that very mission. It is the role of the Christian to witness to Jesus. Whatever our position in this world, we are called to be disciples of Christ. By our words and deeds others should realize that we live in the joy of knowing that Jesus is Lord. We do not have to depend upon our own limited resources, but can draw strength from the vastness of Christ's saving grace.

QUOTE: "They came to John saying, 'Rabbi, the man who was with you across the Jordan—the one about whom you have been testifying—is baptizing now, and everyone is flocking to him.' John answered: 'No one can lay hold on anything unless it is given him from on high. You yourself are witnesses to the fact that I said: I am not the Messiah; I am sent before him. It is the groom who has the bride. The groom's best man waits there listening for him and is overjoyed to hear his voice. That is my joy, and it is complete. He must increase, while I must decrease' " (John 3,26-30).

GREGORY THE GREAT,
pope and doctor
(540?-604)

Coming events cast their shadows before — Gregory was the Prefect of Rome before he was 30. After five years in office, he resigned, founded six monasteries on his Sicilian estate, and became a

Benedictine monk in his own home at Rome.

Ordained a priest, he became one of the Pope's seven deacons, and also served six years in the East as papal nuncio in Constantinople. He was recalled to become abbot, and at the age of 50 was elected pope by the clergy and people of Rome.

He was direct and firm. He removed unworthy priests from office, forbade taking money for many services, emptied the papal treasury to ransom prisoners of the Lombards and to care for persecuted Jews and the victims of plague and famine. He was very concerned about the conversion of England, sending 40 monks from his own monastery. He is known for his reform of the liturgy, for strengthening respect for doctrine. Whether he was largely responsible for the revision of "Gregorian" chant is disputed.

Gregory lived in a time of perpetual strife with invading Lombards and difficult relations with the East. When Rome itself was under attack, it was he who went to interview the Lombard king.

An Anglican historian has written: "It is impossible to conceive what would have been the confusion, the lawlessness, the chaotic state of the middle ages without the medieval papacy; and of the medieval papacy, the real father is Gregory the Great."

His book, *Pastoral Care,* on the duties and qualities of a bishop, was read for centuries after his death. He described bishops mainly as physicians whose main duties were preaching and the enforcement of discipline. In his own down-to-earth preaching, Gregory was skilled at applying the daily

Gospel to the needs of his listeners.

Called "the Great," Gregory has been given a place with Augustine, Ambrose and Jerome as one of the four key Doctors of the Western Church.

COMMENT: Gregory was content to be a monk, but he willingly served the Church in other ways when asked. He sacrificed his own preferences in many ways, especially when he was called to be Bishop of Rome. Once he was called to public service, Gregory gave his considerable energies completely to this work.

QUOTE: "Perhaps it is not after all so difficult for a man to part with his possessions, but it is certainly most difficult for him to part with himself. To renounce what one has is a minor thing; but to renounce what one is, that is asking a lot" (St. Gregory, Homily 32 on the Gospels).

September 9   *Memorial (U.S.A.)*

PETER CLAVER, priest
(1581-1654)

A native of Spain, young Jesuit Peter Claver left his homeland forever in 1610 to be a missionary in the colonies of the New World. He sailed into Cartagena (now in Columbia), a rich port city washed by the Caribbean. He was ordained there in 1615.

By this time the slave trade had been established in the Americas for nearly one hundred years, and Cartegena was a chief center for it. Ten thousand slaves poured into the port each year after crossing the Atlantic from West Africa under conditions so foul and inhuman that an estimated one-third of the passengers died in transit. Although the practice of slave-trading was condemned by Pope Paul III and later labeled "supreme villainy" by Pius IX, it continued to flourish.

Peter Claver's predecessor, Jesuit Father Alfonso de Sandoval, had devoted himself to the service of the slaves for 40 years before Claver arrived to continue his work, declaring himself "the slave of the Negroes forever."

As soon as a slave ship entered the port, Peter Claver moved into its infested hold to minister to the ill-treated and miserable passengers. After the slaves were herded out of the ship like chained animals and shut up in nearby yards to be gazed at by the crowds, Claver plunged in among them with medicines, food, bread, brandy, lemons and tobacco. With the help of interpreters, he gave basic instructions and assured his brothers and sisters of their human dignity and God's saving love. During the 40 years of his ministry, Claver instructed and baptized an estimated 300,000 slaves.

His apostolate extended beyond his care for slaves. He became a moral force, indeed, the apostle of Cartagena. He preached in the city square, gave missions to sailors and traders as well as country missions, during which he avoided, when possible, the hospitality of the planters and owners and lodged in the slave quarters instead.

After four years of sickness which forced the saint to remain inactive and largely neglected, he died on September 8, 1654. The city magistrates, who had previously frowned at his solicitude for the Negro outcasts, ordered that he should be buried at public expense and with great pomp.

He was canonized in 1888, and Pope Leo XIII declared him the worldwide patron of missionary work among Negroes.

COMMENT: The Holy Spirit's might and power is manifested in the striking decisions and bold actions of Peter Claver. A decision to leave one's homeland never to return reveals a gigantic act of will difficult for the contemporary mind to imagine. Peter's determination to serve forever the most abused, repulsed and lowly of all people is stunningly heroic. When we measure our lives against such a man's, we become aware of our own barely used potential and of our need to open ourselves more to the jolting power of Jesus' Spirit.

QUOTE: Peter Claver understood that concrete service like the distributing of medicine, food or brandy to his Negro brothers and sisters could be as effective a communication of the Word of God as was mere *verbal* preaching. As Peter Claver would often say, "We must speak to them with our hands, before we try to speak to them with our lips."

JOHN CHRYSOSTOM,
bishop and doctor
(d. 407)

The ambiguity and intrigue surrounding John, the great preacher (his name means "golden-mouthed") from Antioch, are characteristic of the life of any great man in a capitol city. Brought to Constantinople after a dozen years of priestly service in Syria, John found himself the reluctant victim of an imperial ruse to make him bishop in the greatest city of the empire. Ascetic, unimposing but dignified, and troubled by stomach ailments from his desert days as a monk, John began his episcopate under the cloud of imperial politics.

If his body was weak, his tongue was powerful. The content of his sermons, his exegesis of Sacred Scripture, were never without a point. Sometimes the point stung the high and mighty. Some sermons lasted up to two hours.

His life style at the imperial court was not appreciated by some courtiers. He offered a modest table to episcopal sycophants hanging around for imperial and ecclesiastical favors. John deplored court protocol that accorded him precedence before the highest state officials. He would not be a kept man.

His zeal led him to decisive action. Bishops who bribed their way into their office were deposed. Many of his sermons called for concrete steps to share wealth with the poor. The rich did not appreciate hearing from John that private property existed

because of Adam's fall from grace any more than
married men liked to hear that they too were bound
to marital fidelity just as much as their wives. When
it came to justice and charity, John acknowledged no
double standards.

Aloof, energetic, outspoken, especially when he
became excited in the pulpit, John was a sure target
for criticism and personal trouble. He was accused
of gorging himself secretly on rich wines and fine
foods. His faithfulness as spiritual director to the
rich widow, Olympia, provoked much gossip at-

tempting to prove him a hypocrite where wealth and chastity were concerned. His action taken against unworthy bishops in Asia Minor was viewed by other ecclesiastics as a greedy, uncanonical extension of his authority.

Two prominent personages who personally undertook to discredit John were Theophilus, archbishop of Alexandria, and the Empress Eudoxia. Theophilus feared the growth in importance of the bishop of Constantinople and took occasion to charge John with fostering heresy. Theophilus and other angered bishops were supported by Eudoxia. The Empress resented his sermons contrasting Gospel values with the excesses of imperial court life. Whether intended or not, sermons mentioning the lurid Jezebel and impious Herodias were associated with the Empress, who finally did manage to have John exiled. He died in exile in 407.

COMMENT: John Chrysostom's preaching, by word and example, exemplifies the role of the prophet to comfort the disturbed and to disturb the comfortable. For his honesty and courage he paid the price of a turbulent ministry as bishop, personal vilification and exile.

QUOTE: Bishops "should set forth the ways by which are to be solved very grave questions concerning the ownership, increase, and just distribution of material goods, peace and war, and brotherly relations among all peoples" (Vatican II, Bishops, 12).

CORNELIUS, pope and martyr, and CYPRIAN, bishop and martyr

Cornelius (d. 253)

There was no pope for 14 months after the martyrdom of St. Fabian because of the intensity of the persecution of the Church. During the interval, the Church was governed by a college of priests. St. Cyprian, a friend of Cornelius, writes that he was elected pope "by the judgment of God and of Christ, by the testimony of most of the clergy, by the vote of the people, with the consent of aged priests and of good men."

The greatest problem of Cornelius' two-year term as pope had to do with the sacrament of Penance and centered on the re-admission of Christians who had apostatized during the time of persecution. Two extremes were finally both condemned. Cyprian, primate of Africa, appealed to the Pope to confirm his stand that the relapsed could be reconciled only by the decision of the bishop (against the very indulgent practice of Novatus).

In Rome, however, Cornelius met with the opposite view. After his election, a priest named Novatian (one of those who had governed the Church) had himself consecrated a rival bishop of Rome — the first anti-pope. He denied that the Church had any power to reconcile not only the apostates, but also those guilty of murder, adultery, fornication or second marriage! Cornelius had the support of most

83

of the Church (especially of Cyprian in Africa) in condemning Novatianism, though the sect persisted for several centuries. He held a synod at Rome in 251 and ordered the "relapsed" to be restored to the Church with the usual "medicines of repentance."

The friendship of Cornelius and Cyprian was strained for a time when one of Cyprian's rivals made accusations about him. But the problem was cleared up.

A document from Cornelius shows the extent of organization in the Church at Rome in mid-third century: 46 priests, seven deacons, seven sub-deacons. It is estimated that the number of Christians were totaled about 50,000.

Cornelius died as a result of the hardships of his exile in what is now Civita Vecchia.

COMMENT: It seems fairly true to say that almost every possible false doctrine has been proposed at some time or other in the history of the Church. The third century saw the resolution of a problem we scarcely consider—the penance to be done before sacramental absolution and reconciliation with the Church after mortal sin. Men like Cornelius and Cyprian were God's instruments in helping the Church find a prudent path between extremes of rigorism and laxity. They are part of the Church's ever-living stream of tradition, ensuring the continuance of what was begun by Christ, and evaluating new experiences through the wisdom and experience of those who have gone before (Roliner).

QUOTE: "There is one God and one Christ and but one episcopal chair, originally founded on Peter, by the Lord's authority. There cannot, therefore, be set up another altar or another priesthood. Whatever any man in his rage or rashness shall appoint, in defiance of the divine institution, must be a spurious, profane and sacrilegious ordinance" (St. Cyprian, *The Unity of the Catholic Church*).

Cyprian, (d.258)

Cyprian is important in the development of Christian thought and practice in the third century, especially in northern Africa.

Highly educated, a famous orator, he was converted to Christianity as an adult. He distributed his goods to the poor, and amazed his fellow citizens by making a vow of chastity before his baptism. Within two years he had been ordained priest and was chosen, against his will, as bishop of Carthage (near modern Tunis).

Cyprian complains that the peace the Church had enjoyed had weakened the spirit of many Christians, and had opened the door to converts who did not have the true spirit of faith. When the Decian persecution began, many Christians easily abandoned the Church. It was their reinstatement that caused the great controversies of the third century, and helped the Church progress in its understanding of the sacrament of Penance. Novatus, a priest who had opposed Cyprian's election, set himself up in Cyprian's absence (he had fled to a hiding place from which to direct the Church—bringing criticism on himself) and received back all apostates without imposing any canonical penance. Ultimately he was condemned. Cyprian held a middle course, holding that those who had actually sacrificed to idols could receive communion only at death, whereas those who had only bought certificates saying they had sacrificed could be admitted after a more or less lengthy period of penance. Even this was relaxed during a new persecution.

During a plague in Carthage, he urged Christians to help everyone, including their enemies and persecutors.

A friend of Pope Cornelius, he opposed the following pope, Stephen. He and the other African bishops would not recognize the validity of Baptism conferred by heretics and schismatics. This was not the universal view of the Church, but Cyprian was not intimidated even by Stephen's threat of excommunication.

He was exiled by the emperor and then recalled for trial. He refused to leave the city, insisting that his people should have the witness of his martyrdom.

Cyprian was a mixture of kindness and courage, vigor and steadiness. He was cheerful and serious, so that people did not know whether to love or respect him more. He waxed warm during the baptismal controversy; his feelings must have concerned him, for it was at this time that he wrote his treatise on patience. St. Augustine remarks that Cyprian atoned for his anger by his glorious martyrdom.

COMMENT: The controversies about Baptism and Penance in the third century remind us that the early Church had no ready-made solutions from the Holy Spirit. The leaders and members of the Church of that day had to move painfully through the best series of judgments they could make in an attempt to follow the entire teaching of Christ and not be diverted by exaggerations to right or left.

QUOTE: "You cannot have God for your Father if you do not have the Church for your mother.... God is one and Christ is one, and his Church is one; one is the faith, and one is the people cemented together by harmony into the strong unity of a body.... If we are the heirs of Christ, let us abide in the peace of Christ; if we are the sons of God, let us be lovers of peace" (St. Cyprian, *The Unity of the Catholic Church*).

September 17   *Optional*

ROBERT BELLARMINE,
bishop and doctor
(1542-1621)

When Robert Bellarmine was ordained in 1570, the study of Church history and the Fathers of the Church was in a sad state of neglect. A promising scholar from his youth in Tuscany, he devoted his energy to these two subjects, as well as to Holy Scripture, in order to systematize Church doctrine against the attacks of the Reformers. He was the first Jesuit to become a professor at Louvain.

His most famous work is his three volume *Disputations on the Controversies* of the Christian faith. Particularly noteworthy are the sections on the temporal power of the pope and the role of the laity. He incurred the anger of both England and France by showing the divine-right-of-kings theory as untenable. He developed the theory of the indirect power of the pope in temporal affairs; although he was defending the pope against the Scottish philosopher Barclay, he also incurred the ire of Pope Sixtus V.

Bellarmine was made a cardinal by Pope Clement VIII on the grounds that "he had not his equal for learning." While he occupied apartments in the Vatican, Bellarmine relaxed none of his former austerities. He limited his household expenses to what was barely essential, eating only the food available to the poor. He was known to have ransomed a soldier who had deserted from the army, and he used the hangings of his rooms to clothe poor people, remarking, "the walls won't catch cold."

Among many activities, he became theologian to Pope Clement VIII, preparing two catechisms which have had great influence in the Church.

The last major controversy of Bellarmine's life came in 1616 when he had to admonish his friend Galileo, whom he admired. Bellarmine delivered the admonition on behalf of the Holy Office which had decided that the heliocentric theory of Copernicus was contrary to Scripture. The admonition amounted to a caution against putting forward—other than as a hypothesis—theories not yet fully proved. It was an example of the fact that saints are not infallible.

Bellarmine died on September 17, 1621. The process for his canonization was begun in 1627 but was delayed for political reasons, stemming from his writings, until 1930. In 1931 Pius XI declared him a Doctor of the Church.

COMMENT: The renewal in the Church sought by

Vatican II has been difficult for many Catholics. In the course of change, many of us feel a lack of firm guidance from those in authority. We yearn for the stone columns of orthodoxy and an iron command with clearly defined lines of authority.

Vatican II assures us in *The Church in the Modern World,* "There are many realities which do not change and which have their ultimate foundation in Christ, who is the same yesterday and today, yes, and forever."

Robert Bellarmine devoted his life to the study of Scripture and Catholic doctrine. His writings help us understand that not only is the content of our faith important, it is Jesus' living person—as revealed by his life, death and resurrection—that is the source of revelation.

The real source of our faith is not merely a set of doctrines but rather the person of Christ still living in the Church today. When he left his apostles, Jesus assured them of his living presence: "When the Spirit of truth comes, he will lead you to the complete truth."

QUOTE: "Sharing in solicitude for all the churches, bishops exercise this episcopal office of theirs, received through episcopal consecration, in communion with and under the authority of the Supreme Pontiff. All are united in a college or body with respect to teaching the universal Church of God and governing her as shepherds" (Vatican II, Bishops, 3).

JANUARIUS, bishop and martyr
(d. 305?)

Nothing is known of his life. He is believed to have been martyred in the persecution of Diocletian in 305. *Legend* has it that after he was thrown to the bears in the amphitheater of Pozzuoli, he was beheaded, and his blood ultimately brought to Naples.

COMMENT: It is defined Catholic doctrine that miracles can happen and can be recognized — hardly a mind-boggling statement to anyone who believes in God. Problems arise, however, when we must decide whether an occurrence is *unexplainable* in natural terms, or only *unexplained.* All men do well to avoid an excessive credulity, which may be a sign of insecurity. On the other hand, when even scientists speak about "probabilities" rather than "laws" of nature, it is something less than imaginative for Christians to think that God is so "scientific" that he cannot work *extraordinary* miracles to wake us up to the *everyday* miracles of sparrows and dandelions, raindrops and snowflakes.

QUOTE: *The liquefactions:* According to the *Catholic Encyclopedia:* "A dark mass that half fills a hermetically sealed 4 inch glass container, and is preserved in a double reliquary in the Naples cathedral as the blood of St. January, liquefies 18 times during the year . . . . This phenomenon goes back to the 14th century . . . . Tradition connects it with a certain Eusebia, who had allegedly collected the blood after the martyrdom . . . . The ceremony accompanying the liquefaction is performed by holding the reliquary close to the altar on which is located what is believed to be the martyr's head. While the people pray, often tumultuously, the priest turns the reliquary up and down in the full sight of the onlookers until the liquefaction takes place . . . . Various experiments have been applied, but the phenomenon eludes natural explanation. There are, however, similar miraculous claims made for the blood of John the Baptist, Stephen, Pantaleon, Patricia, Nicholas of Tolentino and Aloysius Gonzaga — nearly all in the neighborhood of Naples."

MATTHEW, apostle and evangelist

Matthew was a Jew who worked for the occupying Roman forces, collecting taxes from his fellow Jews. Though the Romans probably did not allow extremes of extortion, their main concern was their own purses. They were not scrupulous about what the "tax-farmers" got for themselves. Hence the latter, known as "publicans," were generally hated as traitors by their fellow Jews. The Pharisees lumped them with "sinners." So it was shocking to them to hear Jesus call such a man to be one of his intimate followers.

Matthew got Jesus in further trouble by having a

sort of going-away party at his house. The Gospel tells us that "many" tax collectors and "those known as sinners" came to the dinner. The Pharisees were still more badly shocked. What business did the supposedly great teacher have associating with such immoral people? Jesus' answer was, "I have come to help sinners, not the self-righteous who (think they) don't need help. Go and learn what this means: 'I desire mercy — love of neighbor for the sake of God — and not sacrifice.'" Jesus is not setting aside ritual and worship; he is saying that loving others is even more important.

No other particular incidents about Matthew are found in the New Testament.

COMMENT: From such an unlikely situation, Jesus chose one of the foundations of the Church, a man who others, judging from his job, thought was not holy enough for the position. But he was honest enough to admit that he was one of the sinners Jesus came to call. He was open enough to recognize truth when he saw him. "He got up and followed him."

STORY: We imagine Matthew, after the terrible events surrounding the death of Jesus, going to the mountain to which the Risen One had summoned them. "At the sight of him, those who had entertained doubts (apparently this included all of them) fell down in homage. Jesus came forward and addressed them in these words: (we think of him looking at each one in turn, Matthew listening and excited with the rest) 'Full power is given me in heaven and on earth. You go, therefore, and make disciples of all nations. Baptize them in the name of the

Father and of the Son and of the Holy Spirit. Teach them to carry out everything I have commanded you. And I am with you always, until the end of the world.' " Matthew would never forget that day. He proclaimed the Good News by his life and by his word. Our faith rests upon his witness and that of his fellow apostles.

September 26   *Optional*

COSMAS and DAMIAN, martyrs
(d. 303?)

Nothing is known of their lives except that they suffered martyrdom in Syria during the persecution of Diocletian.

A church erected on the site of their burial place was enlarged by the Emperor Justinian. Devotion to the two saints spread rapidly in both East and West. A famous basilica was erected in their honor in Constantinople. Their names were placed in the canon of the Mass, probably in the sixth century.

Legend says that they were twin brothers born in Arabia, who became skilled doctors. They were among those who are venerated in the East as the "moneyless ones" because they did not charge a fee for their services. It was impossible that such prominent persons would escape unnoticed in time of persecution: they were arrested and beheaded.

COMMENT: For a long time, it seems, we have been very conscious of Jesus' miracles as proofs of his divinity. What we sometimes overlook is Jesus' consuming interest in simply *healing* people's sickness, whatever other meaning his actions had. The power that "went out from him" was indeed a sign that God was definitively breaking into human history in final fulfillment of his promises; but the love of God was also concrete in a very human heart that was concerned about the suffering of his brothers and sisters. It is a reminder to Christians that salvation is for the whole *person*, the unique body-spirit unity.

QUOTE: "You must know that your body is a temple of the Holy Spirit, who is within — the Spirit you have received from God. You are not your own. You have been purchased, and at a price. So glorify God in your body" (I Cor. 6,19).

September 27   *Memorial*

VINCENT DE PAUL, priest
(1580?-1660)

The deathbed confession of a dying servant opened Vincent's eyes to the crying spiritual needs of the peasantry of France. This seems to have been a crucial moment in the life of the man from a small farm in Gascony, France, who had become a priest with little more ambition than to have a comfortable life.

It was the Countess de Gondi (whose servant he had helped) who persuaded her husband to endow and support a group of able and zealous missionaries who would work among the poor, the vassals and te-

94

nants, and the country people in general. Vincent was too humble to accept leadership at first, but after working for some time in Paris among imprisoned galley-slaves, he returned to be the leader of what is now known as the Congregation of the Mission, or the Vincentians. These priests, with vows of poverty, chastity, obedience and stability, were to devote themselves entirely to the people in smaller towns and villages.

Later Vincent established confraternities of charity for the spiritual and physical relief of the poor and sick of each parish. From these, with the help of Saint Louise de Marillac, came the Sisters of Charity, "whose convent is the sickroom, whose chapel is the parish church, whose cloister is the streets of the city." He organized the rich women of Paris to collect funds for his missionary projects, founded several hospitals, collected relief funds for the victims of war, and ransomed over 1200 galley slaves from North Africa. He was zealous in conducting retreats for clergy at a time when there was great laxity, abuse and ignorance among them. He was a pioneer in clerical training and was instrumental in establishing seminaries.

Most remarkably, Vincent was by temperament a very irascible person — even his friends admitted it. He said that except for the grace of God he would have been "hard and repulsive, rough and cross." But he became a tender and affectionate man, very sensitive to the needs of others.

Pope Leo XIII made him the patron of all charitable societies. Outstanding among these, of course, is the Society of St. Vincent de Paul, founded in 1833 by his admirer Frederic Ozanam.

COMMENT: The Church is for all God's children, rich and poor, peasants and scholars, the sophisticated and the simple. But obviously the greatest concern of the Church must be for those who need the most help — those made helpless by sickness, poverty, ignorance or cruelty. Vincent de Paul is a particularly appropriate patron for all Christians today, when hunger is becoming starvation, and the high living of the rich stands in more and more glaring contrast to the physical and moral degradation in which many of God's children are forced to live.

QUOTE: "Strive to live content in the midst of those things that cause your discontent."

"Free your mind from all that troubles you, God will take care of things. You will be unable to make haste in this (choice) without, so to speak, grieving the heart of God, because he sees that you do not honor him sufficiently with holy trust. Trust in him, I beg you, and you will have the fulfillment of what your heart desires" (Letters).

September 28   *Optional*

WENCESLAUS, martyr
(907?-929)

If saints have been falsely characterized as "otherworldly," the life of Wenceslaus stands as an example to the contrary: he stood for Christian values in the midst of the political intrigues which characterized 10th century Bohemia.

He was born in 907 near Prague, son of the Duke of Bohemia. His saintly grandmother, Ludmilla, raised him and sought to promote him as ruler of Bohemia in place of his mother, who favored the anti-Christian factions. Ludmilla was eventually murdered, but rival Christian forces were victorious, and Wenceslaus was able to assume leadership of the government.

His rule was marked by efforts toward unification within Bohemia, support of the Church, and peace-making negotiations with Germany, a policy which caused him trouble with the anti-Christian opposition. His brother Boleslav joined in the plotting, and in September of 929 invited Wenceslaus to Alt-Bunglou for the celebration of the feast of Sts. Cosmas and Damian. On the way to Mass, Boleslav attacked his brother, and in the struggle, Wenceslaus was killed by supporters of Boleslav.

Although his death resulted primarily from political upheaval, Wenceslaus was hailed as a martyr for the faith, and his tomb became a pilgrimage shrine. He is hailed as the patron of the Bohemian people and of modern Czechoslovakia.

COMMENT: "Good King Wenceslaus" was able to incarnate his Christianity in a world filled with political unrest. While we are often victims of violence of a different sort, we can easily identify with his struggle to bring harmony to society. The call to become involved in social change, and in political activity, is addressed to Christians; the values of the Gospel are sorely needed today.

QUOTE: "While recognizing the autonomy of the reality of politics, Christians who are invited to take up political activity should try to make their choices consistent with the Gospel and, in the framework of a legitimate plurality, to give both personal and collective witness to the seriousness of their faith by effective and disinterested service of men" (Pope Paul VI, "A Call to Action," 46).

September 30   *Memorial*

JEROME, priest and doctor
(345 - 420 A.D.)

Most of the saints are remembered for some outstanding virtue or devotion which they practiced, but Jerome is remembered too frequently for his bad temper! It is true that he had a very bad temper and could use a vitriolic pen, but his love for God and his Son Jesus Christ was extraordinarily intense; anyone who taught error was an enemy of God and truth, and St. Jerome went after him with his mighty and sometimes sarcastic pen.

He was above all a Scripture scholar, translating the Old Testament from the Hebrew and the New Testament from the Greek. He also wrote commentaries which are a great source of scriptural inspiration for us today. He was an avid student, a thorough scholar, a prodigious letter writer and a consultant for monk, bishop and pope. St. Augustine said of him, "What Jerome is ignorant of, no mortal has ever known."

St. Jerome is particularly important for having made a translation of the bible which came to be called the Vulgate. It is not the most critical edition of the bible, but its acceptance by the Church was fortunate. As a modern scholar says, "No man before Jerome or among his contemporaries and very few men for many centuries afterwards were so well qualified to do the work." The Council of Trent called for a new and corrected edition of the Vulgate, and declared it to be the authentic text to be used in the Church.

In order to be able to do such work, he prepared himself well. He was a master in Latin, Greek, Hebrew and Chaldaic. He began his studies at his birthplace, Stridon in Dalmatia (now Jugoslavia). After his preliminary education he went to Rome, the center of learning at that time, and thence to Trier, Germany, where the scholar was very much in evidence. He spent several years in each place trying always to find the very best teachers.

After these preparatory studies he traveled extensively in Palestine, marking each spot of Christ's life with an outpouring of his devotion. Mystic that he was, he spent five years in the desert of Chalcis so that he might give himself up to prayer, penance and study. Finally he settled in Bethlehem where he lived in the cave believed to have been the birthplace of Christ. On September 30, 420, Jerome died in Bethlehem. The remains of his body now lie buried in the Basilica of St. Mary Major in Rome.

COMMENT: Jerome was a strong, outspoken man. He had the virtues and the unpleasant fruits of being a fearless critic and all the usual moral problems of a man. He was, as someone had said, no admirer of moderation whether in virtue or against evil. He was swift to anger, but also swift to remorse, even more severe on his own shortcomings than on those of others. A pope is said to have remarked, on seeing a picture of Jerome striking his breast with a stone, "You do well to carry that stone, for without it the Church would never have canonized you" *(Butler's Lives of the Saints)*.

QUOTE: "In the remotest part of a wild and stony desert, burnt up with the heat of the scorching sun so that it frightens even the monks that inhabit it, I seemed to myself to be in the midst of the delights and crowds of Rome. In this exile and prison to which for the fear of hell I had voluntarily condemned myself, I many times imagined myself witnessing the dancing of the Roman maidens as if I had been in the midst of them: in my cold body and in my parched-up flesh, which seemed dead before its death, passion was able to live. Alone with this enemy, I threw myself in spirit at the feet of Jesus, watering them with my tears, and I tamed my flesh by fasting whole weeks. I am not ashamed to disclose my temptations, but I grieve that I am not now what I then was" (Letter to St. Eustochium).

October 1   *Memorial*

THERESE OF THE CHILD JESUS, virgin
(1873 - 1897)

"I prefer the monotony of obscure sacrifice to

all ecstasies. To pick up a pin for love can convert a soul." These are the words of Therese of the Child Jesus, a Carmelite nun who lived a cloistered life of obscurity in the convent of Lisieux, France. And her preference for hidden sacrifice did indeed convert souls. Few saints of God are more popular than this young nun. Her autobiography, *The Story of a Soul,* is read and loved throughout the world. Therese Martin entered the convent at the age of 15 and died in 1897 at the age of 24.

Life in a Carmelite convent is indeed uneventful and consists mainly of prayer and hard domestic work. But Therese possessed that holy insight that redeems the time, however dull that time may be. She saw in quiet suffering *redemptive suffering,* suffering that was indeed her apostolate. Therese said she came to the Carmel Convent "to save souls and pray for priests." And shortly before she died, she wrote: "I want to spend my heaven doing good on earth."

COMMENT: Therese has much to teach our age of the image, the appearance, the "sell." We have become a dangerously self-conscious people, painfully aware of the need to be fulfilled, yet knowing we are not. Therese, like so many saints, sought to serve others, to do something outside herself, to forget herself in quiet acts of love. She is one of the great examples of the Gospel paradox that we gain our life by losing it, and that the seed that falls into the ground must die in order to live.

Preoccupation with self separates modern man from God, from his fellows, and ultimately from himself. He must re-learn to forget himself, to contemplate a God who draws him out of himself, and to serve others as the ultimate expression of selfhood. These are the insights of St. Therese of Lisieux, and they are more valid today than ever.

QUOTE: All her life long St. Therese suffered from illness. As a young girl she underwent a three-month malady characterized by violent crises, extended delirium, and prolonged fainting spells. Afterwards she was ever frail and yet she worked hard in the laundry and refectory of the convent. Psychologically, she endured prolonged periods of darkness when the light of faith seemed all but extinguished. The last year of her life she slowly wasted away from tuberculosis. And yet shortly before her death on September 30 she murmured, "I would not suffer less."

Truly she was a valiant woman, who did not whimper about her illnesses and anxieties. Here was a person who saw the power of love, that divine alchemy which can change everything, including weakness and illness, into service and redemptive power for others. Is it any wonder that she is patroness of the missions? Who else but those who embrace suffering with their love really convert the world?

October 4   *Memorial*

FRANCIS OF ASSISI
(1181? - 1226)

Francis of Assisi was a poor little man who as-

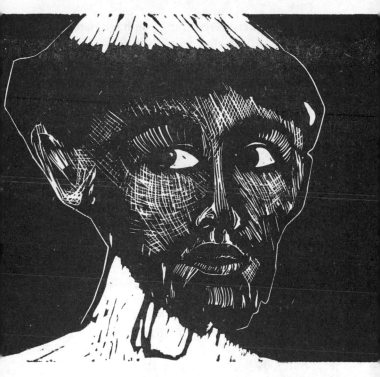

tounded and inspired the Church by taking the Gospel *literally*, not in a narrow fundamentalist sense, but by actually following all that Jesus said and did, joyfully, without limit and without a mite of self-importance.

Serious illness brought the young Francis to see the emptiness of his frolicking life as leader of Assisi's youth. Prayer — lengthy and difficult — led him to a self-emptying like that of Christ, climaxed by his embracing a leper he met on the road. It symbolized his complete obedience to what he had heard in prayer: "Francis! Everything you have loved and desired in the flesh it is your duty to despise and hate, if you wish to know my will. And when you have begun this, all that now seems sweet and lovely to you will become intolerable and bitter, but all that you used to avoid will turn itself to great sweetness and exceeding joy."

From the cross in the neglected field-chapel of San Damiano, Christ told him, "Francis, go out and build up my house, for it is nearly falling down." Francis became the totally poor and humble workman.

He must have suspected a deeper meaning to "build up my house." But he would have been content to be for the rest of his life the poor "nothing" man actually putting brick on brick in abandoned chapels. He gave up every material thing he had, piling even his clothes before his earthly father (who was demanding restitution for Francis' "gifts" to the poor) so that he could be totally free to say "Our Father in heaven." He was, for a time, considered to be a religious "nut," begging from door to door when he could not get money for his work, bringing sadness or disgust to the hearts of his former friends, ridicule from the unthinking.

But genuineness will tell. A few people began to realize that this man was actually trying to be Christian. He really believed what Jesus said: "Announce the kingdom! Don't possess gold or silver or copper in your purses, no traveling bag, no sandals, no staff."

Francis' first Rule for his followers was a collection of texts from the Gospel. He had no idea of founding an order, but once it began he protected it, and accepted all the legal structures needed to support it. His devotion and loyalty to the Church was absolute, and highly exemplary at a time when various movements of reform tended to break her unity.

He was torn between a life devoted entirely to prayer and a life of active preaching of the Good News. He decided in favor of the latter, but always returned to solitude when he could. He wanted to be a missionary in Syria, in Africa, but was prevented by shipwreck and illness in both cases. He did manage to try to convert the Sultan of Egypt during the Fifth Crusade.

During the last years of his relatively short life (he died at 44) he was half-blind and seriously ill. Two years before his death, he received the stigmata, the real and painful wounds of Christ in his hands, feet and side.

On his deathbed, he said over and over again the last addition to his Canticle of the Sun, "Be praised, O Lord, for our Sister Death." He sang the 141st Psalm, and at the end asked his superior to have his clothes removed when the last hour came, and received permission to expire lying naked on the earth, in imitation of his Lord.

COMMENT: Francis of Assisi was poor only that he might be Christlike. He loved nature because it was another manifestation of the beauty of God. He did great penance (apologizing to "Brother Body" later in life) that he might be totally disciplined for the will of God. His poverty had a sister, humility, by which he meant total dependence on the good God.

But all this was, as it were, preliminary to the heart of his spirituality: living the Gospel life, summed up in the charity of Jesus, and perfectly expressed in the Eucharist.

QUOTE: "We adore you, and we bless you Lord Jesus Christ, here and in all the churches which are in the whole world, because by your Holy Cross you have redeemed the world" (St. Francis).

October 6   *Optional*

BRUNO, priest
(1030? - 1101)

This saint has the honor of having founded a religious order which, as the saying goes, has never had to be *re*formed because it was never *de*formed. No doubt both the founder and the members would reject such high praise, but it is an indication of the saint's intense love of a penitential life in solitude.

He was born in Cologne, became a famous teacher at Rheims, and was appointed chancellor of the archdiocese at the age of 45. He supported Pope Gregory VII in his fight against the decadence of the clergy, and took part in the removal of his own scandalous archbishop Manasses. Bruno suffered the plundering of his house for his pains.

He had a dream of living in solitude and prayer, and persuaded a few friends to join him in a hermitage. After a while he felt the place unsuitable, and through a friend was given some land which was to become famous for his foundation — in the

Chartreuse (from which comes the word Carthusians). The climate, desert, mountainous terrain and inaccessibility guaranteed silence, poverty and small numbers.

They built an oratory with small individual cells at a distance from each other. They met for Matins and Vespers each day, and spent the rest of the time in solitude, eating together only on great feasts. Their chief work was copying manuscripts.

The Pope, hearing of Bruno's holiness, called for his assistance in Rome. When the Pope had to flee Rome, Bruno pulled up stakes again, and spent his last years (after refusing a bishopric) in the wilderness of Calabria.

He was never formally canonized, because the Carthusians were averse to all occasions of publicity. Pope Clement extended his feast to the whole Church in 1674.

COMMENT: If there is always a certain uneasy questioning of the contemplative life, there is an even greater puzzlement about the extremely penitential combination of community and hermit life lived by the Carthusians.

QUOTE: "Members of those communities which are totally dedicated to contemplation give themselves to God alone in solitude and silence and through constant prayer and ready penance. No matter how urgent may be the needs of the active apostolate, such communities will always have a distinguished part to play in Christ's Mystical Body" (Vatican II, Religious Life, 7).

DENIS, bishop and martyr, and COMPANIONS, martyrs
(d. 258?)

This martyr and patron of France is traditionally held to have been the Denis of Paris, first bishop of Paris. His popularity is due to a series of legends, especially those connecting him with the great abbey church of St. Denis in Paris. He was for a time confused with the writer now called Pseudo-Dionysius.

The best hypothesis contends that Denis was sent to Gaul from Rome in the third century and beheaded in the persecution under Valerius in 258.

According to one of the legends, after he was martyred on Montmartre (literally "Mountain of martyrs") in Paris, he carried his head to a village northeast of the city. St. Genevieve built a basilica over his tomb at the beginning of the sixth century.

COMMENT: Again we have the case of a saint about which almost nothing is known, yet one whose cult has been a vigorous part of the Church's history for centuries. We can only conclude that the deep impression the saint made on the people of his day must have resulted from a life of unusual holiness. In all such cases, there are two fundamental facts: a great man gave his life for Christ, and the Church has never forgotten him — a human symbol of the eternal mindfulness of our Father.

QUOTE: "Martyrdom is part of the Church's nature

since it manifests Christian death in its pure form, as the death of unrestrained faith, which is otherwise hidden in the ambivalence of all human events. Through martyrdom the Church's holiness, instead of remaining purely subjective, achieves by God's grace the visible expression it needs. As early as the second century one who accepted death for the sake of Christian faith or Christian morals was looked on and revered as a "martus" (witness). The term is scriptural in that Jesus Christ is the "faithful witness" absolutely [Rev. 1,5;3,14] (Karl Rahner, *Theological Dictionary*).

October 9   *Optional*

JOHN LEONARDI, priest
(1541? - 1609)

"I am only one person!" "Why should I do anything?" "What good would it do?" Today, as in any age, man seems plagued with the dilemma of getting involved. In his own way John Leonardi answered these questions. As one person, he chose to become a priest.

After his ordination, he became very active in the works of the ministry, especially in hospitals and prisons. The example and dedication of his work attracted several young laymen who began to assist him. They later became priests themselves.

John lived in a time of reform after the Reformation and the Council of Trent. He and his followers projected a new congregation of diocesan priests. For some reason the plan, which was ultimately approved, provoked great political opposition; and he was an exile from his home town of Lucca, Italy, for almost the entire remainder of his life. He received encouragement and help from St. Philip Neri (May 26) who gave him his quarters — along with the care of his cat!

In 1579 he formed the Confraternity of Christian Doctrine, and published a compendium of Christian doctrine that remained in use until the 19th century.

Father Leonardi and his priests became a great power for good in Italy, and their congregation was confirmed by Pope Clement in 1595. He died at the age of 68 from a disease caught when tending those stricken by the plague.

By the deliberate policy of the founder, the Clerks Regular of the Mother of God have never had more than 15 churches, and today form only a very small congregation.

COMMENT: What can one man do? If you ever glanced through a *Christopher Notes* pamphlet you know — plenty! In the life of each saint one thing stands clear: God and one are a majority! What one man, following God's will and plan for his life, can do is more than our mind could ever hope for or imagine. Each of us, like John Leonardi, have a mission to fulfill in God's plan for the world. Each one of us is unique, and has been given talent to use for the service of our brothers and sisters for the building up of God's Kingdom.

QUOTE: "Do not live in fear, little flock. It has

pleased your Father to give you the kingdom. Sell what you have and give alms. Get purses for yourselves that do not wear out, a never-failing treasure with the Lord which no thief comes near nor any moth destroys" (Luke 12,32-33).

October 14   *Optional*

CALLISTUS I, pope and martyr
(d. 223?)

The most reliable information about this saint comes from his enemy, St. Hippolytus, (August 13) the first anti-pope, later a martyr for the Church. A negative principle is used: if some worse things had happened, Hippolytus would surely have mentioned them.

Callistus was a slave in the imperial Roman household. Put in charge of the bank by his master, he lost the money deposited, fled and was caught. After serving time for a while, he was released to make some attempt to recover the money. Apparently he carried his zeal too far, being arrested for brawling in a Jewish synagogue. This time he was condemned to work in the mines of Sardinia. He was released through the influence of the Emperor's mistress and lived at Anzio (site of a famous World War II beachhead).

He won his freedom, was made superintendent of the public Christian burial ground in Rome (still called the cemetery of St. Callistus), probably the first land owned by the Church. The Pope ordained him a deacon, made him his friend and adviser.

He was himself elected pope by a majority vote of the clergy and laity of Rome, and thereafter was bitterly attacked by the losing candidate, St. Hippolytus, who let himself be set up as the first antipope in the history of the Church. The schism lasted about 18 years.

Hippolytus is venerated as a saint. He was banished during the persecution of 235 and was reconciled to the Church. He died from his sufferings in Sardinia. He attacked Callistus on two fronts — doctrine and discipline. Hippolytus seems to have exaggerated the distinction between Father and Son (almost making two gods) possibly because theological language had not yet been refined. He also accused Callistus of being too lenient, for reasons we may find surprising: 1) he admitted to communion those who had already done public penance for murder, adultery, fornication; 2) he held marriages between free women and slaves to be valid — contrary to Roman law; 3) he authorized the ordination of men who had been married two or three times; 4) he held that mortal sin was not a sufficient reason to depose a bishop; 5) he held to a policy of leniency toward those who had temporarily apostatized during persecution.

Callistus was martyred during a local disturbance in Trastevere, Rome, and is the first pope, except for Peter, to be commemorated as a martyr in the earliest martyrology of the Church.

Some are of the opinion that, even from the little we know about him, Callistus may rank among the greatest popes.

COMMENT: The life of this man is another reminder that the course of Church history, like that of true love, never did run smooth. The Church had to (and still must) go through the agonizing struggle to state the mysteries of the faith in language that, at the very least, sets up definite barriers to error. On the disciplinary side, the Church had to preserve the mercy of Christ against rigorism while still upholding the Gospel ideal of radical conversion and self-discipline. Every pope — indeed every Christian — must walk the difficult path between "reasonable" indulgence and "reasonable" rigorism.

QUOTE: Jesus said, these people "are like children squatting in the town squares, calling to their playmates, 'We piped a (happy) tune but you did not dance! We sang a dirge but you did not wail!' In other words, John (the Baptist) appeared neither eating nor drinking, and people say, 'He is mad!' The Son of Man appeared eating and drinking, and they say, 'This one is a glutton and drunkard, a lover of tax collectors and those outside the law!' " (Mt. 11,16-19).

TERESA OF AVILA, virgin and doctor
(1515-1582)

Teresa lived in an age of exploration as well as political, social and religious upheaval. It was the 16th century, an age of turmoil and reform. Her life began with the culmination of Protestant reform,

and ended shortly after the council of Trent.

The gift of God to Teresa in and through which she became holy, and left her mark on the Church and the world, is threefold: she was a woman; she was a contemplative; she was an active reformer.

As a woman, Teresa stood on her own two feet, even in the man's world of her time. She was "her own woman," entering the Carmelite Order despite strong opposition from her father. She is a person wrapt not so much in silence as in mystery. Beautiful, talented, outgoing, adaptable, affectionate, courageous, enthusiastic, she is totally human, and womanly. Like Jesus, she is a mystery of paradoxes: wise, yet practical; intelligent, yet much in tune with her experience; mystic, yet an energetic reformer. A holy woman, a womanly woman.

Teresa was a woman "for God," a woman of prayer, discipline and compassion. Her heart belonged to God. Her own conversion was no overnight affair; it was an arduous lifelong struggle, involving ongoing purification and suffering. She was misunderstood, misjudged, opposed in her efforts at reform. Yet she struggled on, courageous and faithful; she struggled with her own mediocrity, her illness, her opposition. And in the midst of all this she clung to God in life and prayer. Her writings on prayer and contemplation are drawn from her experience: powerful, practical and graceful. A woman of prayer; a woman for God.

Teresa was a woman "for others." Though a contemplative she spent much of her time and energy seeking to reform herself and the Carmelites, to lead them back to the full observance of the primitive rule. She founded over a half-dozen new monasteries. She traveled, wrote, fought — always to renew, to reform. In her self, in her prayer, in her life, in her efforts at reform, in all the people she touched, she was a woman for others, a woman who inspired and gave life.

COMMENT: Today we live in a time of turmoil, a time of reform and a time of liberation. Supporters of Women's Liberation have in Teresa a challenging example. Promoters of renewal, promoters of prayer, all have in Teresa a woman to reckon with, one whom they can admire and imitate.

QUOTE: Teresa knew well the continued presence and value of suffering (physical illness, opposition to reform, difficulties in prayer), but she grew to be able to embrace suffering, even desire it: "Lord, either to suffer or to die." Toward the end of her life: "Oh, my Lord! how true it is that whoever works for you is paid in troubles! And what a precious price to those who love you if we understand its value."

October 16   *Optional*

HEDWIG, religious
(1174?-1243)

Far too rarely do humans realize the possibilities of the wise use of earthly power and worldly wealth. Hedwig was one of the few. Born to nobility toward the close of the 12th century, she was given in marriage at an early age to Henry, Duke of Silesia. Through her persuasion and personal efforts, a large number of monastic institutions of both men and women were established in Silesia. Several hospitals, one for lepers, were likewise founded. She was personally a great force in establishing peace in the surrounding areas in those troubled times of power struggles. To her great sorrow, she was unable to prevent a pitched battle between the forces of two of her sons, one of whom was dissatisfied over the partition of estates that Henry had made between them.

After she and her husband had made a mutual

vow of continence, she lived, for the most part, at the monastery at Trebnitz, where, although not a formal member of the religious institute, she nevertheless participated in the religious exercises of the community. She died in 1243 and was buried at Trebnitz.

COMMENT: Whatever possessions we may be blessed with are not for our own needs or personal comfort alone, but are also to be used in the assistance of others. To whatever use these goods may be put, they should always promote, never impede, progress in God's love. It is true that earthly things of themselves in no way contradict God's love, but rather are evidences of it; still, we can become so interested in and enticed by what we sense that we become forgetful of the God from whom these blessings come.

STORY: Hedwig sacrificed her wish to become a religious in later life in order that she might use earthly goods to help the poor. For herself, she chose poverty, distrusting the comforts her means might have afforded her and denying herself even basic necessities, e.g., shoes in winter. She wore the religious habit, lived the life of a religious, but would not give up the administration of her possessions because she wanted these goods to help the poor. She lived her life and used whatever goods were hers so that she and those she was able to help might better appreciate the supernatural life of God's grace.

MARGARET MARY ALACOQUE,
virgin
(1647-1690)

Margaret Mary was chosen by Christ to arouse the Church to a realization of the love of God symbolized by the heart of Jesus.

Her early years were marked by sickness and a painful home situation. "The heaviest of my crosses was that I could do nothing to lighten the cross my mother was suffering." After considering marriage for some time, she entered the Order of Visitation nuns at the age of 24.

A Visitation nun was "*not* to be extraordinary except by being ordinary," but the young nun was not to enjoy this anonymity. A fellow novice (shrewdest of critics) termed Margaret humble, simple and frank, but above all kind and patient under sharp criticism and correction. She could not meditate in the formal way expected, though she tried her best to give up her "prayer of simplicity." Slow, quiet and clumsy, she was assigned to help an infirmarian who was a bundle of energy.

On December 27, 1674, three years a nun, she received the first of her revelations. She felt "invested" with the presence of God, though always afraid of deceiving herself in such matters. The request of Christ was that his love for mankind be made evident through her. During the next 13 months, he appeared to her at intervals. His human heart was to be the symbol of his divine-human love.

By her own love she was to make up for the coldness and ingratitude of the world — by frequent and loving Holy Communion, especially on the first Friday of each month, and by an hour's vigil of prayer every Thursday night in memory of his agony and isolation in Gethsemane. He also asked that a feast of reparation be instituted.

Like all saints, Margaret had to pay for her gift of holiness. Some of her own sisters were hostile. Theologians who were called in declared her visions delusions, and suggested that she eat more heartily. Later, parents of children she taught called her an imposter, an unorthodox innovator. A new confessor, Blessed Claude de la Colombiere, a Jesuit, recognized her genuineness and supported her. Against her great resistance, Christ called her to be a sacrificial victim for the shortcomings of her own sisters, and to make this known.

After serving as novice mistress and assistant superior, she died at the age of 43, while being anointed. "I need nothing but God, and to lose myself in the heart of Jesus."

COMMENT: Our scientific-materialistic age cannot "prove" private revelations. Theologians, if pressed, admit that we do not "have" to believe in them. But it is impossible to deny the message Margaret Mary heralded: that God loves us with a passionate love. Her insistence on reparation and prayer, and the reminder of final judgment should be sufficient to ward off superstition and superficiality in devotion to the Sacred Heart while preserving its deep Christian meaning.

QUOTE: Christ speaks to St. Margaret Mary (Third apparition): "Behold this Heart which has so loved men that it has spared nothing, even to exhausting and consuming itself, in order to testify its love. In return, I receive from the greater part only ingratitude, by their irreverence and sacrileges, and by the coldness and contempt they have for me in this Sacrament of love . . . I come into the heart I have given you in order that through your fervor you may atone for the offences which I have received from lukewarm and slothful hearts that dishonor me in the Blessed Sacrament."

October 17   *Memorial*

IGNATIUS OF ANTIOCH,
bishop and martyr
(d. 107?)

Born in Syria, Ignatius converted to Christianity and eventually became bishop of Antioch. In the year 107 the emperor Trajan visited Antioch and forced the Christians there to choose between death and apostasy. Ignatius would not deny Christ and thus was condemned to be put to death in Rome.

Ignatius is well known for the seven letters he wrote on the long journey from Antioch to Rome. Five of these letters are to Churches in Asia Minor and urge the Christians there to remain faithful to God and to obey their superiors; he warns them against heretical doctrines, providing them with the solid truths of the Christian faith.

The sixth letter was to Polycarp, bishop of Smyrna, who was later martyred for the faith. The final letter begs the Christians in Rome not to try to stop his martyrdom. "The only thing I ask of you is to allow me to offer the libation of my blood to God. I am the wheat of the Lord, may I be ground by the teeth of the beasts to become the immaculate bread of Christ."

In the year 107 Ignatius bravely met the lions in the Coliseum.

COMMENT: Ignatius' great concern was for the unity and order of the Church. Even greater was his willingness to suffer martyrdom rather than deny his Lord Jesus Christ. Not to his own suffering did Ignatius draw attention but to the love of God which strengthened him. He knew the price of commitment and would not deny Christ, even to save his own life.

QUOTE: "I greet you from Smyrna together with the Churches of God present here with me. They comfort me in every way, both in body and in soul. My chains, which I carry about on me for Jesus Christ, begging that I may happily make my way to God, exhort you: persevere in your concord and in your community prayers" (Ignatius of Antioch, *Letter to the Church at Tralles*).

October 18   *Feast*

LUKE, evangelist

Luke wrote one of the major portions of the New Testament, a two-volume work comprising the third

Gospel and the Acts of the Apostles. In the two books he shows the parallel between the life of Christ and that of the Church. He is the only gentile Christian among the Gospel writers. Tradition holds him to be a native of Antioch, and Paul calls him "our beloved physician" (Col. 4, 14). His Gospel was probably written between 70 and 85 A.D.

He appears in Acts during Paul's second journey, remains at Philippi for several years until Paul returns from his third journey, accompanies Paul to Jerusalem and remains near him when he is imprisoned in Caesarea. During these two years, Luke had time to seek information and interview persons who had known Jesus. He accompanied Paul on the dangerous journey to Rome where he is a faithful companion. "Only Luke is with me," Paul writes (2 Tim. 4,11).

COMMENT: Luke wrote as a gentile for gentile Christians. He attempted to render Jesus comprehensible to Greek Christians. The Gospel reveals Luke's expertise in classic Greek style as well as his knowledge of Jewish sources.

The character of Luke may best be seen by the emphases of his Gospel, which has been given a number of subtitles: 1) The Gospel of Mercy. Luke emphasizes Jesus' compassion and patience with the sinners and the suffering. He has a broadminded openness to all, showing concern for Samaritans, lepers, publicans, soldiers, public sinners, unlettered shepherds, the poor. He alone records the parable of the sinful woman, the lost sheep and coin, the prodigal son, the good thief. 2) The Gospel of

Universal Salvation. Jesus died for all men. He is the son of Adam, not just of David, and the gentiles are his friends too. 3) The Gospel. of the Poor. "Little people" are prominent: Zechariah and Elizabeth, Mary and Joseph, shepherds, Simeon, and the elderly widow, Anna. He is also concerned with what we now call "evangical poverty." 4) The Gospel of Absolute Renunciation. He stresses the need of total dedication to Christ. 5) The Gospel of Prayer and the Holy Spirit. He shows Jesus at prayer before every important step of his ministry. The Spirit is bringing the Church to its final perfection. 6) The Gospel of Joy. Luke succeeds in portraying the joy of salvation that permeated the primitive Church.

QUOTE: The end of Luke's Gospel: "Then Jesus led them out near Bethany, and with hands upraised, blessed them. As he blessed, he left them, and was taken up to heaven. They fell down to do him reverence, then returned to Jerusalem filled with joy. There they were to be found in the temple constantly, speaking the praises of God."

OCTOBER 19   *Memorial*

ISAAC JOGUES and
JOHN DE BREBEUF,
priests and martyrs, and
COMPANIONS, martyrs

Isaac Jogues (1607-1646)

Isaac Jogues and his companions were the first

martyrs of the North American continent. As a young Jesuit, Isaac Jogues, a man of learning and culture, taught literature in France. He gave up that career to work among the Huron Indians in the New World, and in 1636 he and his companions, under the leadership of John de Brebeuf, arrived in Quebec. The Hurons were constantly warred upon by the Iroquois, and in a few years Father Jogues was captured by the Iroquois and imprisoned for 13 months. His letters and journals tell how he and his companions were led from village to village, how they were beaten, tortured, and forced to watch as their Huron converts were mangled and killed. An unexpected chance for escape came to Isaac Jogues through the Dutch, and he returned to France, bearing the marks of his sufferings. Several fingers had been cut, chewed, or burnt off. Pope Urban VIII gave him permission to offer Mass with his mutilated hands: "It would be shameful that a martyr of Christ be not allowed to drink the blood of Christ." Welcomed home as a hero, Father Jogues might have sat back, thanked God for his safe return, and died peacefully in his homeland. But his zeal led him back once more to the fulfillment of his dreams. In a few months he sailed for his missions among the Hurons.

In 1646 he and Jean de Lalande, who had offered his services to the missioners, set out for Iroquois country in the belief that a recently signed peace treaty would be observed. They were captured by a Mohawk war party, and on October 18 Father Jogues was tomahawked and beheaded. Jean de Lalande was killed the next day at Ossernenon, a village near Albany, New York.

The first of the Jesuit missionaries to be martyred was Rene Goupil who, with Lalande, had offered his services as an oblate. He was tortured along with Isaac Jogues in 1642, and was tomahawked for having made the sign of the cross on the brow of some children.

John de Brebeuf (1593-1649)

Jean de Brebeuf was a French Jesuit who came to Canada at the age of 32 and labored there for 24 years. He returned to France when the English captured Quebec in 1629 and expelled the Jesuits, but returned to his missions four years later. An epidemic of smallpox among the Hurons was blamed on the Jesuits by the medicine men, but Jean remained with them.

He composed catechisms and a dictionary in Huron, and saw 7,000 converted before his death. He was captured by the Iroquois and died after four hours of extreme torture at Sainte Marie, near Georgian Bay, Canada.

Father Anthony Daniel, working among Hurons who were gradually becoming Christian, was killed by Iroquois on July 4, 1648. His body was thrown into his chapel, which was set on fire.

Gabriel Lalemant had taken a fourth vow — to sacrifice his life to the Indians. He was horribly tortured to death along with Father Brebeuf.

Father Charles Garnier was shot to death as he baptized children and catechumens during an Iroquois attack.

Father Noel Chabanel was killed before he

could answer his recall to France. He had found it exceedingly hard to adapt to mission life: he could not learn the language, the food and life of the Indians revolted him, and he suffered spiritual dryness during his whole stay in Canada. Yet he made a vow to remain until death in his mission.

These eight Jesuit martyrs of North America were canonized in 1930.

COMMENT: Faith and heroism planted belief in Christ's cross deep in our land. The Church in North America sprang from the blood of martyrs. Are we as eager to keep that cross standing in our midst? Do we bear witness to the deep-seated faith in us, carrying the good news of the cross (redemption) into our home, our work, our social world?

QUOTE: "My confidence is placed in God who does not need our help for accomplishing his designs. Our single endeavor should be to give ourselves to the work and to be faithful to him, and not to spoil his work by our shortcomings." (From a letter of Isaac Jogues to a Jesuit friend in France, September 12, 1646, a month before he died.)

PAUL OF THE CROSS, priest
(1694-1775)

Paul Francis is known as a mystic, missionary, spiritual director and founder of the Passionists. The second of 16 children, Paul had to discontinue his education at a boarding school in Genoa in order to help support his family.

A leader by nature, strong-willed but gentle, Paul easily won the confidence of his contemporaries. His biographers record that along with the compassion he naturally felt for the physical and spiritual poverty of others, he also had an equally strong attraction toward contemplation, solitude and penance. After living for some time as a hermit, he founded in Rome the Passionist Congregation, which is devoted to preaching in parish missions or renewals of the mystery of the cross.

Above all else Paul is the mystic of the cross. One biographer records that nothing was more contemporary to him than the passion of Christ.

Paul fully exemplified the primary apostolate of his congregation — the preaching of the Word. The parish mission was for him a confrontation of the Christian with Christ in the paradox of the cross. This confrontation evoked a commitment to crucifixion in the continuing passion of Christ and its redemptive work in the daily lives of his hearers.

In order to arrive at this commitment, Paul developed a mission method that involved the laity in an active role in processions, street preaching, vigils, penitential works and sacrifices, hymns, prayers, and at times in the sermon itself.

Paul died in Rome on October 18, 1775, and was canonized by Pius IX on June 29, 1867.

COMMENT: "If anyone wishes to come after me, let him deny himself, take up his cross daily and follow me" (Luke 9,23). Jesus was known for his

127

"hard sayings." He clashed so sharply with the powerful interests of the world that he ran the risk of the cross — the designated punishment for those whom Rome saw as a threat.

Paul of the Cross helps us realize that "carrying the cross" often means voluntary suffering, for it may lead to less of those goods of the world so prized by most men. But what reward is there? Jesus says "rejoice and exult" when you are persecuted because this means intimate personal association with himself and other dedicated human beings like him. These people have the joy of being other Christs and the real transforming agents of the world today.

STORY: When, cross in hand, with arms out-stretched, he preached about the sufferings of Christ, his words seemed to pierce the stoniest hearts; and when he scourged himself in public for the offences of the people, hardened soldiers and even bandits wept, confessing their sins.

"Father, I have been in great battles without ever flinching at the cannon's roar," exclaimed a soldier who was attending one of the missions. "But when I listen to you I tremble from head to foot."

Afterwards in the confessional Paul would deal tenderly with his penitents, confirming them in their good resolutions, leading them on to amendment of life and suggesting practical aids to perseverance.

JOHN OF CAPISTRANO, priest
(1386-1456)

It has been said that Christian saints are the world's greatest optimists. Not blind to the existence and consequences of evil, they base their confidence on the power of Christ's redemption. The power of conversion through Christ extends not only to sinful people but also to calamitous events.

Imagine being born in the 14th century. One-third of the population and nearly 40 per cent of the clergy were wiped out by the Black Death. The Western Schism split the Church with two or three claimants to the Holy See at one time. England and France were at war. The city-states of Italy were constantly in conflict. No wonder that gloom was the spirit of the culture and the times.

John Capistrano was born in 1386. His education was thorough. His talents and success were great. When he was 26 he was made governor of Perugia. Imprisoned after a battle against the Malatestas, he resolved to change his way of life completely. At the age of 30 he entered the Franciscan novitiate and was ordained priest in four years.

His preaching attracted great throngs at a time of religious apathy and confusion. He and 12 Franciscan brethren were received in the countries of central Europe as angels of God. They were instrumental in reviving a dying faith and devotion.

The Franciscan Order itself was in turmoil over

the interpretation and observance of the Rule of St. Francis. Through John's tireless efforts and his expertise in law, the heretical Fraticelli were suppressed and the "Spirituals" were freed from interference in their stricter observance.

He helped bring about a reunion with the Greek and Armenian Churches, unfortunately only a brief arrangement.

When the Turks captured Constantinople, he was commissioned to preach a crusade for the defense of Europe. Gaining little response in Bavaria and Austria, he decided to concentrate his efforts in Hungary. He himself led the army to Belgrade. Under the great general John Junyadi they gained an overwhelming victory, and the siege of Belgrade was lifted. Worn out by his superhuman efforts Capistrano was an easy prey to the infection bred by the refuse of battle. He died October 23, 1456.

COMMENT: John Hofer, a biographer of John Capistran, recalls a Brussels organization, named after the saint, which aims at solving life problems in a fully Christian spirit. Its motto was the three words, Initiative, Organization, Activity. These truly are most characteristic of John's life. He was not one to sit around, period. His deep Christian optimism drove him to battle problems at all levels with the confidence engendered by a deep faith in Christ.

QUOTE: On the saint's tomb in the Hungarian town of Villach, the governor had this message inscribed: "This tomb holds John, by birth of Capistrano, a man worthy of all praise, defender and promoter of the faith, guardian of the Church, zealous protector of his Order, an ornament to all the world, lover of truth and justice, mirror of life, surest guide in doctrine; praised by countless tongues, he reigns blessed in heaven." That's a fitting epitaph for a real and successful optimist.

October 24   *Optional*

ANTHONY CLARET, bishop
(1807-1870)

The "Spiritual Father of Cuba" was a missionary, religious founder, social reformer, queen's chaplain, writer and publisher, archbishop and refugee. He was a Spaniard whose work took him to the Canary Islands, Cuba, Madrid, Paris and to the First Vatican Council.

In his spare time as weaver and designer in the textile mills of Barcelona, he learned Latin and printing: the future priest and publisher was preparing. Ordained at 28, he was prevented by ill health from entering religious life both as a Carthusian and as a Jesuit, and went on to become one of Spain's most popular preachers. He spent 10 years in giving popular missions and retreats, always placing great emphasis on the Eucharist and devotion to the Immaculate Heart of Mary. Her rosary, it was said, was never out of his hand. At 42, beginning with five young priests, he founded a religious institute of missionaries, known today as the Claretians.

He was appointed to head the much-neglected

archdiocese of Santiago in Cuba. He began its reform by almost ceaseless preaching and hearing of confessions, and suffered bitter opposition — mainly for stamping out concubinage and giving instruction to Negro slaves. A hired assassin (whose release from prison Anthony had obtained) slashed open his face and wrist. Anthony succeeded in getting his death sentence commuted to a prison term. His solution for the misery of Cubans was family-owned farms producing a variety of foods for the family's own needs and for the market. This invited the enmity of the vested interests who wanted everyone to work on a single cash crop — sugar. Amid all his religious writing, it is interesting to note the titles of two books he wrote in Cuba: *Reflections on Agriculture* and *Country Delights*.

He was called back to Spain for a job he did not relish — being chaplain for the queen. He went, on three conditions: he would reside away from the palace, he would come only to hear the queen's confession and instruct the children, and he would be exempt from court functions. In the revolution of 1868, he fled with the queen's party to Paris, where he preached to the Spanish colony.

All his life Anthony was interested in the Catholic Press. He founded the Religious Publishing House, a major Catholic publishing venture in Spain, and wrote or published 200 books and pamphlets.

At Vatican I, where he was a staunch defender of the doctrine of infallibility, he won the admiration of his fellow bishops. Cardinal Gibbons of Baltimore remarked of him, "There goes a true saint." He died in exile near the border of Spain at the age of 63.

COMMENT: Jesus foretold that those who are truly representative of him would suffer the same persecution as he did. Besides 14 attempts on his life, Anthony had to undergo such a barrage of the ugliest slander that the very name "Claret" became a byword for humiliation and misfortune. The powers of evil do not easily give up their prey.

No one needs to go looking for persecution. All we need to do is be sure we suffer because of our genuine faith in Christ, not for our own whims and imprudences.

STORY: Queen Isabella II once said to Anthony, her chaplain, "No one tells me things as clearly and frankly as you do." Later, "Everybody is always asking me for favors, but you never do. Isn't there something you would like for yourself?" He replied, "Yes, that you let me resign." The queen made no more offers.

October 28   *Feast*

SIMON and JUDE, apostles

Jude is so named by Luke and Acts. Matthew and Mark call him Thaddeus. He is not mentioned elsewhere in the Gospels, except, of course, where all the apostles are referred to. Scholars hold that he is not the author of the epistle of Jude. Actually, "Jude" had the same name as "Judas" Iscariot. Evidently because of the disgrace of that name, it was shortened to "Jude" in English.

Simon is mentioned on all four lists of the apostles. On two of them he is called "the Zealot." The Zealots were a Jewish sect which represented an extreme of Jewish nationalism. For them, the messianic promise of the Old Testament meant that the Jews were to be a free and independent nation. God alone was their king, and any payment of taxes to the Romans — the very domination of the Romans — was a blasphemy against God. No doubt some of the Zealots were the spiritual heirs of the Maccabees, carrying on their ideals of religion and independence. But many were the counterparts of modern terrorists. They raided and killed, attacking both foreigners and "collaborating" Jews. They were chiefly responsible for the rebellion against Rome which ended in the destruction of Jerusalem in 70 A.D.

COMMENT: As in the case of all the apostles except for Peter, James and John, we are faced with men who are really unknown, and we are struck by the fact that their holiness is simply taken to be a gift of Christ. He chose some unlikely people: a former Zealot, a former (crooked) tax collector, an impetuous fisherman, two "sons of thunder" and a man named Judas Iscariot.

It is a reminder that we cannot receive too often. Holiness does not depend on human merit, culture, personality, effort or achievement. It is entirely God's creation and gift.

God needs no Zealots to bring about the

kingdom by force. Jude, like all the saints, is the saint of the impossible: only God can create his divine life in men. And he wills to do so, for all of us.

QUOTE: "Just as Christ was sent by the Father, so also he sent the apostles, filled with the Holy Spirit. This he did so that, by preaching the Gospel to every creature, they might proclaim that the Son of God, by his death and resurrection, had freed us from the power of Satan and from death, and brought us into the kingdom of his Father" (Vatican II, Liturgy, 6).

November 3 *Optional*

MARTIN de PORRES, religious
(1579-1639)

"Father unknown" is the cold legal phrase for it on baptismal records. "Half-breed" or "war souvenir" is the cruel name inflicted by those of "pure" blood. Like many others, Martin might have grown to be a bitter man, but he did not. It was said that even as a child he gave his heart and his goods to the poor and despised.

He was the illegitimate son of a freed-woman of Panama, probably a Negro but possibly of Indian stock, and a Spanish grandee of Lima, Peru. He inherited the features and dark complexion of his mother; and though this irked his father, he finally acknowledged his son after eight years. After the birth of a sister, he abandoned the family. Martin was reared in poverty, locked into a low level of Lima's society.

At 12 his mother apprenticed him to a barber-surgeon. He learned how to cut hair and also how to draw blood (a standard medical treatment then), care for wounds, and prepare and administer medicines.

After a few years in this medical apostolate, he applied to the Dominicans to be a "lay helper," not feeling himself worthy to be a religious brother. After nine years, the example of his prayer and penance, charity and humility led the community to request him to make full religious profession. Many of his nights were spent in prayer and penitential practices; his days were filled with nursing the sick, caring for the poor. It was particularly impressive that he treated all men regardless of their color, race or status. He was instrumental in founding an orphanage, took care of slaves brought from Africa, and managed the daily alms of the priory with practicality as well as generosity. He became the procurator for both priory and city whether it was a matter of "blankets, shirts, candles, candy, miracles or prayers!" When his priory was in debt, he said, "I am only a poor mulatto. Sell me. I am the property of the Order. Sell me."

Side by side with his daily work in the kitchen, laundry and infirmary, God chose to fill Martin's life with extraordinary gifts: ecstasies that lifted him into the air, light filling the room where he prayed, bilocation, miraculous knowledge, instantaneous cures and a remarkable control over animals. His charity extended to beasts of the field and even to the vermin of the kitchen. He would excuse the raids of mice and rats on the ground that they were underfed, and kept stray cats and dogs at his sister's house.

He became a formidable fund-raiser, obtaining thousands of dollars for dowries for poor girls, so that they could marry or enter a convent.

Many of his fellow religious took him as their spiritual director, but he continued to call himself a "poor slave." He was a good friend of another Dominican saint of Peru, Rose of Lima.

COMMENT: Racism is a sin almost nobody confesses. Like pollution, it is a "sin of the world" that is everybody's responsibility but apparently nobody's fault. One could hardly imagine a more fitting patron of Christian forgiveness (on the part of those discriminated against) and Christian justice (on the part of reformed racists) than Martin de Porres.

QUOTE: Pope John XXIII at the canonization of Martin, May 6, 1962, remarked, "He excused the faults of others. He forgave the bitterest injuries, convinced that he deserved much severer punishments on account of his own sins. He tried with all his might to redeem the guilty; lovingly he comforted the sick; he provided food, clothing and medicine for the poor; he helped, as best he could, farm laborers and Negroes, as well as mulattoes, who were looked upon at that time as akin to slaves: thus he deserved to be called by the name the people gave him: *Martin of Charity*."

CHARLES BORROMEO, bishop
(1538-1584)

The name of St. Charles Borromeo is associated with reform. He lived during the time of the Protestant Reformation, and had a hand in the reform of the Archdiocese of Milan as well as the reform of the whole Church during the final years of the Council of Trent.

Although he belonged to a noble Milanese family and was related to the powerful Medici family, he desired to devote himself to the Church. When his uncle, Cardinal de Medici, was elected pope in 1559 as Pius IV, he made Charles cardinal-deacon and administrator of the archdiocese of Milan while he was still a layman and a young student. Because of his intellectual qualities he was entrusted with several important offices connected with the Vatican and later appointed Secretary of State with full charge of the administration of the papal states. The untimely death of his elder brother brought Charles to a definite decision to be ordained a priest, despite relatives' insistence that he marry. He was ordained priest at the age of 25, and soon afterward he was consecrated bishop of Milan.

But because of his work at the Council of Trent he was not allowed to take up residence in Milan until the Council was over. It had been Charles who encouraged the Pope to renew the Council in 1562 after it had been suspended 10 years before. Working behind the scenes, St. Charles deserves the credit for keeping the Council in session when at several points it was on the verge of breaking up. He took upon himself the task of the entire correspondence during the final phase. Eventually St. Charles was allowed to devote all his time to the archdiocese of Milan. The religious and moral picture was far from bright. The reform needed in every phase of Catholic life among both clergy and laity was initiated at a Provincial Council of all his suffragan bishops. Specific regulations were drawn up for bishops and other clergy· if the people were to be converted to a better life, these had to be the first to give a good example and renew their apostolic spirit.

St. Charles himself took the initiative in giving good example. He allotted most of his income to charity, forbade himself all luxury, imposed severe penances upon himself. He sacrificed wealth, high honors, esteem and influence to become poor. During the plague and famine of 1576 he tried to feed 60,000 to 70,000 people daily. To do this he borrowed large sums of money that required years to repay. When the civil authorities fled at the height of the plague, he stayed in the city where he ministered to the sick and the dying, and helped those in want.

Work and heavy burdens of his high office began to affect his health. He died at the age of 46.

COMMENT: St. Charles made his own the words of Christ: "I was hungry and you gave me to eat; I was thirsty and you gave me to drink; I was a stranger and you took me in; naked and you covered me; sick and you visited me; I was in prison and you came to me" (Mt. 25,35-37). St. Charles saw Christ in his neighbor and knew that his charity for the least of his flock was charity done for Christ.

QUOTE: "Christ summons the Church, as she goes her pilgrim way, to that continual reformation of which she always has need, insofar as she is an institution of men here on earth. Therefore, if the influence of events of the times has led to deficiences in conduct, in Church discipline, or even in the formulation of doctrine (which must be carefully distinguished from the deposit of faith itself), these should be appropriately rectified at the proper moment" (Vatican II, Ecumenism, 6).

LEO THE GREAT, pope and doctor
(d. 461)

With apparent strong conviction of the importance of the Bishop of Rome in the Church, and the Church as the ongoing sign of Christ's presence in the world, Leo the Great displayed endless dedication in his role as pope. Elected in 440, he worked tirelessly as "Peter's successor," guiding his fellow bishops as "equals in the episcopacy and infirmities."

Leo is known as one of the best administrative popes of the ancient Church. His work branched into four main areas, indicative of his notion of the pope's total responsibility for the flock of Christ. He worked at length to control the heresies of Pelagianism, Manichaeism and others, placing demands on their followers so as to secure true Christian beliefs. A second major area of his concern was doctrinal controversy in the Church in the East, to which he responded with a classic letter setting down the Church's teaching of the nature of Christ. With strong faith, he also led the defense of Rome against barbarian attack, taking the role of peacemaker.

In these three areas, Leo's work has been highly regarded. His growth to sainthood has its basis in the spiritual depth with which he approached the pastoral care of his people, which was a fourth focus of his work. He is known for his spiritually profound sermons. An instrument of the call to holiness, well versed in Scripture and ecclesiastical awareness, Leo had the ability to reach the everyday needs and interests of his people. One of his Christmas sermons is still famous today.

COMMENT: At a time when there is widespread criticism of structure in the Church, we also hear criticism that bishops and priests — indeed, all of us — are too preoccupied with administration of temporal matters. Pope Leo is an example of a great administrator who used his talents in areas where spirit and structure are inseparably combined: doctrine, peace and pastoral care. He avoided an "angelism" that tries to live without the body, as well as a "practicality" that deals only in externals.

STORY: It is said of Leo that his true significance rests in his doctrinal insistence on the mysteries of Christ and the Church and in the supernatural charisms of the spiritual life given to man in Christ and in his body the Church. Thus Leo held firmly that

141

everything he did and said as pope for the administration of the Church was participated in by Christ, the head of the mystical body, and by St. Peter, in whose place Leo acted.

MARTIN OF TOURS, bishop
(316?-397)

A conscientious objector who wanted to be a monk; a monk who was maneuvered into being a bishop; a bishop who fought paganism as well as pleaded for mercy to heretics; such was Martin of Tours, one of the most popular of saints.

He was born of pagan parents in what is now Hungary and raised in Italy. The son of a veteran, he was forced to serve in the army against his will at the age of 15. He became a Christian catechumen, and was baptized at 18. It was said that he lived more like a monk than a soldier. At 23, he refused a war-bounty from Julian Caesar with the words, "I have served you as a soldier; now let me serve Christ. Give the bounty to those who are going to fight. But I am a soldier of Christ and it is not lawful for me to fight." After great difficulties, he was discharged, and went to be a disciple of Hilary of Poitiers.

He was ordained an exorcist and worked with great zeal against the Arians. He became a monk, living first at Milan and later on a small island. When Hilary was restored to his see after exile, Martin returned to France and established what may have been the first French monastery, near Poitiers. He lived there for 10 years, forming his disciples and preaching throughout the countryside.

The people of Tours demanded that he become their bishop. He was drawn to that city by a ruse — the need of a sick person — and was brought to the Church, where reluctantly he allowed himself to be consecrated bishop. Some of the consecrating bishops thought his rumpled appearance and unkempt hair indicated that he was not dignified enough for the office.

Along with St. Ambrose, he rejected Bishop Ithacius' principle of putting heretics to death — as well as the intrusion of the emperor into such matters. He prevailed upon the emperor to spare the life of the heretic Priscillian. For his efforts, Martin was accused of the same heresy, and Priscillian was executed. Martin then pleaded for a cessation of the persecution of Priscillian's followers in Spain. He still felt he could cooperate with Ithacius in other areas, but afterwards his conscience troubled him about this decision.

As death approached, his followers begged him not to leave them. He prayed, "Lord, if your people still need me, I do not refuse the work. Your will be done."

COMMENT: Martin's worry about cooperation reminds us that almost nothing is either all black or all white. The saints are not creatures of another world: they face the same perplexing decisions that we do. Any decision of conscience always involves some risk. If we choose to go north, we may never know what would have happened had we gone east, west or south. A hyper-cautious withdrawal from all perplexing situations is not the virtue of prudence; it is, in fact, a bad decision, for "not to decide is to decide."

STORY: On a bitterly cold day, the famous legend goes, Martin met a poor man, almost naked, trembling in the cold and begging from passersby at the city gate. Martin had nothing but his weapons and his clothes. He drew his sword, cut his cloak into two pieces, gave one to the beggar and wrapped himself in the other half. Some of the bystanders laughed at his now odd appearance; others were ashamed at not having relieved the man's misery. That night in his sleep Martin saw Christ dressed in the half of the garment he had given away, and heard him say: "Martin, still a catechumen, has covered me with this garment."

JOSAPHAT, bishop and martyr
(1580?-1623)

In 1967, newspaper photos of Pope Paul VI embracing Athenagoras I, the Orthodox patriarch of Constantinople, marked a significant step toward the healing of a division in Christendom that has spanned nine centuries.

In 1595, when today's saint was a boy, the Orthodox bishop of Brest-Litovsk (famous in World War I) in Lithuania and five other bishops representing millions of Ruthenians, sought reunion with Rome. John Kunsevich (Josaphat became his name in religious life) was to dedicate his life, and suffer his death, in the same cause. Born in what was then Poland, he went to work in Wilno and was influenced by clergy adhering to the Union of Brest. He became a Basilian monk, then a priest, and soon was well known as a preacher and as an ascetic.

He became bishop of Vitebsk (now in Russia) at a relatively young age, and faced a difficult situation. Most religious, fearing interference in liturgy and customs, did not want union with Rome. By synods, catechetical instruction, reform of the clergy and personal example however, Josaphat was successful in winning the greater part of the Orthodox in Lithuania to the union.

But the next year a dissident hierarchy was set up, and his opposite number spread the accusation that Josaphat had "gone Latin" and that all his people would have to do the same. He was not enthusiastically supported by the Latin bishops of Poland.

Despite warnings, he went to Vitebsk, still a hotbed of trouble. Attempts were made to foment trouble and drive him from the diocese: a priest was sent to shout insults to him from his own courtyard. When Josaphat had him removed and shut up in his house, the opposition rang the town hall bell, and a mob assembled. The priest was released, but members of the mob broke into the bishop's home. He was brained with a halberd, then shot, and his body thrown into the river. It was later recovered and is now buried at Biala, Poland. He was the first saint of the Eastern Church to be canonized.

His death brought a movement toward Catholicism and unity, but the controversy continued, and the dissidents, too, had their martyr. After the partition of Poland, the Russians forcibly joined a majority of the Ruthenians to the Orthodox Church of Russia.

COMMENT: The seeds of separation were sown in the fourth century when the Roman Empire was divided into East and West. The actual split came over relatively unimportant customs (unleavened bread, Saturday fasting, celibacy); no doubt the political involvement of religious leaders on both sides was a large factor; and doctrinal disagreement was present. But no reason was enough to justify the present tragic division in Christendom, which is 64 per cent Roman Catholic, 13 per cent Separated Eastern Churches (mostly Orthodox) and 23 per cent Protestant — and this when the 71 per cent of the world that is not Christian should be getting the witness of unity and Christlike charity from Christians!

STORY: Surrounded by an angry mob shortly before his death, Josaphat said, "You people of Vitebsk want to put me to death. You make ambushes for me everywhere, in the streets, on the bridges, on the highways, and in the market place. I am here among you as your shepherd and you ought to know that I should be happy to give my life for you. I am ready to die for the holy union, for the supremacy of St. Peter and of his successor the Supreme Pontiff."

146

FRANCES XAVIER CABRINI, virgin
(1850-1917)

Frances Xavier Cabrini was the first United States citizen to be canonized. Her deep trust in the loving care of her God gave her the strength to be a valiant woman doing the work of Christ.

Refused admission to the religious order which had educated her to be a teacher, she began charitable work at the House of Providence Orphanage in Cadogno, Italy. In September, 1877, she made her vows there and took the religious habit.

When the bishop closed the orphanage in 1880, he named Frances prioress of the Missionary Sisters of the Sacred Heart. Seven young women from the orphanage joined with her.

Since her early childhood in Italy, Frances had wanted to be a missionary in China; but at the urging of Pope Leo XIII, Frances went west instead of east. She traveled with six sisters to New York City to work with the thousands of Italian immigrants living there.

She found disappointment and difficulties with every step. When she arrived in New York City, the house that was to be her first orphanage in the United States was not available. The archbishop advised her to return to Italy. But Frances, truly a valiant woman, departed from the archbishop's residence all the more determined to establish the orphanage. And she succeeded.

In 35 years Frances Xavier Cabrini founded 67

institutions dedicated to caring for the poor, the abandoned, the uneducated and the sick. Seeing great need among Italian immigrants who were losing their faith, she organized schools and adult education classes.

As a child, she was always frightened of water, unable to overcome her fear of drowning. Yet, despite this fear, she traveled across the seas more than 30 times. She died of malaria in her own Columbus Hospital in Chicago.

COMMENT: The compassion and dedication of Mother Cabrini is still seen in hundreds of thousands of her fellow citizens, not yet canonized, who care for the sick in hospitals, nursing homes and state institutions. We complain of increased medical costs in an affluent society; but the daily news shows us millions who have little or no medical care, and who are calling for new Mother Cabrinis to become citizen-servants of their land.

QUOTE: At her canonization on July 7, 1946, Pius XII said, "Although her constitution was very frail, her spirit was endowed with such singular strength that, knowing the will of God in her regard, she permitted nothing to impede her from accomplishing what seemed beyond the strength of a woman."

ALBERT THE GREAT,
bishop and doctor
(1206-1280)

Albert the Great was a 13th-century German Dominican who influenced decisively the stance of the Church toward Aristotelian philosophy brought to Europe by the spread of Islam.

Students of philosophy know him as the master of Thomas Aquinas. Albert's attempt to understand Aristotle's works established the climate in which Thomas Aquinas developed his synthesis of Greek wisdom and Christian theology. But Albert deserves recognition on his own merits as a curious, honest and diligent scholar.

He was the eldest son of a powerful and wealthy German lord of military rank. He was educated in the liberal arts, and despite fierce family opposition, he entered the Dominican novitiate.

His boundless interests prompted him to write a compendium of all knowledge: natural science, logic, rhetoric, mathematics, astronomy, ethics, economics, politics and metaphysics. His explanation of learning took 20 years to complete. "Our intention," he said, "is to make all the aforesaid parts of knowledge intelligible to the Latins."

He achieved his goal while serving as an educator at Paris and Cologne, as Dominican provincial, and even as bishop of Regensburg for a time. He defended the mendicant orders and preached the Crusade to Germany and Bohemia.

Albert is a doctor of the Church and the patron of scientists and philosophers.

COMMENT: An information glut faces us Christians today in all branches of learning. One needs only to read current Catholic periodicals to experience the varied reactions to the findings of the social sciences, for example, in regard to Christian institutions, Christian lifestyles and Christian theology, ultimately, In canonizing Albert, the Church seems to point to his openness to truth, wherever it may be found, as his claim to holiness. His characteristic curiosity prompted Albert to mine deeply for wisdom within a philosophy his Church warmed to with great difficulty.

QUOTE: "There are some who desire knowledge merely for its own sake; and that is shameful curiosity. And there are others who desire to know, in order that they may themselves be known; and that is vanity, disgraceful too. Others again, desire knowledge in order to acquire money or preferment by it; that too is a discreditable quest. But there are also some who desire knowledge, that they may build up the souls of others with it; and that is charity. Others, again, desire it that they may themselves be built up thereby; and that is prudence. Of all these types, only the last two put knowledge to the right use." (St. Bernard: *Sermon on the Canticle of Canticles*).

MARGARET OF SCOTLAND
(1050?-1093)

Margaret of Scotland was a truly liberated woman in the sense that she was free to be herself. For her, that meant freedom to love God and serve others.

Margaret was not Scottish by birth, but Hungarian. Her family fled from William the Conqueror and was shipwrecked off the coast of Scotland. King Malcolm befriended them and was captivated by the beautiful, gracious Margaret. They were married at the castle of Dunfermline in 1070.

Malcolm was goodhearted, but rough and uncultured, as was his country. Because of Malcolm's love for Margaret, she was able to soften his temper, polish his manners and help him become a virtuous king. He left all domestic affairs to her and often consulted her in state matters.

Margaret tried to improve her adopted country by promoting the arts and education. For religious reform, she instigated synods and was present for the discussions which tried to correct religious abuses common among priests and people, such as simony, usury and incestuous marriages. With her husband, she founded several churches.

Margaret was not only a queen, but a mother. She and Malcolm had six sons and two daughters. Margaret personally supervised their religious instruction and their other studies.

Although she was very much caught up in the

affairs of a household and country, she remained detached from the world. Her private life was austere. She had certain times for prayer and reading Scripture. She ate sparingly and slept little in order to have time for devotions. She and Malcolm kept two Lents, one before Easter and one before Christmas. During these times she always rose at midnight for Mass. On the way home she would wash the feet of six poor persons and give them alms. She was always surrounded by beggers in public and never refused them. It is recorded that she never sat down to eat without first feeding nine orphans and 24 adults.

In 1093, King William Rufus made a surprise attack on Alnwick castle. King Malcolm and his oldest son, Edward, were killed. Margaret, already on her deathbed, died four days after her husband.

COMMENT: There are two ways to be charitable: the "clean way" and the "messy way." The "clean way" is to give money or clothing to organizations which serve the poor. The "messy way" is dirtying your own hands in personal service to the poor. Margaret's outstanding virtue was her love of the poor. Although very generous with material gifts, Margaret also visited the sick and nursed them with her own hands. She and her husband served orphans and the poor on their knees during Advent and Lent. Like Christ, she was charitable the "messy way."

QUOTE: "When she (Margaret) spoke, her conversation was seasoned with the salt of wisdom. When she was silent, her silence was filled with good thoughts. So thoroughly did her outward bearing correspond with the staidness of her character that it seemed as if she has been born the pattern of a virtuous life" (Turgot, confessor of St. Margaret).

November 16   *Optional*

GERTRUDE, virgin
(1256?-1302)

St. Gertrude was one of the great mystics of the 13th century. Together with St. Mechtild, she practiced a spirituality called nuptial mysticism, i.e., she came to see herself as the bride of Christ. Her spiritual life was a deep personal union with Jesus and his Sacred Heart, leading her into the very life of the Trinity.

But this was no individualistic piety. Gertrude lived the rhythm of the liturgy, where she found Christ. In the liturgy and Scripture, she found the themes and images to enrich and express her piety. There was no clash between her personal prayer life and the liturgy.

COMMENT: Gertrude's life is another reminder that the heart of the Christian life is prayer: private and liturgical, ordinary or mystical, always personal.

QUOTE: "Lord, you have granted me your secret friendship by opening the sacred ark of your divinity, your deified heart, to me in so many ways as to be the source of all my happiness; sometimes imparting it freely, sometimes as a special mark of our mutual friendship. You have so often melted my soul with your loving caresses that, if I did not know the abyss of your overflowing condescensions, I should be amazed were I told that even your Blessed Mother had been chosen to receive such extraordinary marks of tenderness and affection" (Adapted from *The Life and Revelations of Saint Gertrude, Part II*, Chapter 23).

November 17   *Memorial*

ELIZABETH OF HUNGARY, religious
(1207-1231)

In her short life Elizabeth manifested such great love for the poor and suffering that she has become the patroness of Catholic charities and of the Franciscan Third Order. The daughter of the king of Hungary, Elizabeth chose a life of penance and asceticism when a life of leisure and luxury could easily have been hers. This choice endeared her in the hearts of the common people throughout Europe.

At the age of 14 Elizabeth was married to Louis of Thuringia (a German principality), whom she deeply loved, and bore three children. Under the spiritual direction of a Franciscan friar, she led a life of prayer, sacrifice and service of the poor and sick. Seeking to become one with the poor, she wore simple clothing. Daily she would take bread to hundreds of the poorest in the land who came to her gate.

After six years of marriage, her husband died in the Crusades, and she was grief-stricken. Her husband's family looked upon her as squandering the royal purse, and mistreated her, finally throwing her out of the palace. The return of her husband's allies from the Crusades resulted in her being reinstated, since her son was legal heir to the throne.

In 1228 Elizabeth joined the Third Order of St. Francis, spending the remaining few years of her life caring for the poor in a hospital which she founded in honor of St. Francis. Elizabeth's health declined, and she died before her 24th birthday in 1231. Her great popularity resulted in her canonization four years later.

COMMENT: Elizabeth understood well the lesson Jesus taught when he washed his disciples' feet at the Last Supper: the Christian must be one who serves the humblest needs of others, even if one serves from an exalted position. Of royal blood, Elizabeth could have lorded it over her subjects. Yet she served them with such a loving heart that her brief life won for her a special place in the hearts of many. Elizabeth is also an example to us in her following the guidance of a spiritual director. Growth in the spiritual life is a difficult process. We can play games very easily if we don't have someone to challenge us or share experiences so as to help us avoid pitfalls.

QUOTE: "In our times a special obligation binds us to make ourselves the neighbor of absolutely every person, and of actively helping him when he comes across our path, whether he be an old person abandoned by all, a foreign laborer unjustly looked down upon, a refugee, a child born of an unlawful union and wrongly suffering for a sin he did not commit, or a hungry person who disturbs our conscience by recalling the voice of the Lord: 'As long as you did it for one of these, the least of my brothers, you did it for me' (Mt. 25-40)" (Vatican II, The Church Today, 27).

CECILIA, virgin and martyr

Although Cecilia is one of the most famous of the Roman martyrs, the familiar stories about her are apparently not founded on authentic material. There is no trace of honor being paid her in early times. A fragmentary inscription of the late fourth century refers to a church named after her, and her feast was celebrated at least in 545.

According to legend, Cecilia was a young Christian of high rank betrothed to a Roman named Valerian. Through her influence Valerian was converted, and was martyred along with his brother. The legend about Cecilia's death says that after being struck three times on the neck with a sword, she lived for three days, and asked the pope to convert her home into a church.

Since the time of the Renaissance she has usually been portrayed with a viola or a small organ.

COMMENT: Like any good Christian, Cecilia sang in her heart, and sometimes with her voice. She has become a symbol of the Church's conviction that good music is an integral part of the liturgy, of greater value to the Church than any other art. In the present confused state of church music, it may be useful to recall some words of Vatican II.

QUOTE: "Liturgical action is given a more noble form when sacred rites are solemnized in song, with the assistance of sacred ministers and the active participation of the people . . . . Choirs must be diligently promoted, but bishops and other pastors must ensure that, whenever the sacred action is to be celebrated with song, the whole body of the faithful may be able to contribute that active participation which is rightfully theirs . . . . Gregorian chant, other things being equal, should be given pride of place in liturgical services. But other kinds of sacred music, especially polyphony, are by no means excluded . . . . Religious singing by the people is to be skillfully fostered, so that in devotions and sacred exercises, as also during liturgical services, the voices of the faithful may ring out" (Vatican II, Liturgy, 112-118).

November 23   *Optional*

CLEMENT I, pope and martyr

Clement of Rome was the third successor of St. Peter and reigned as pope during the last decade of the first century. History tells us that he died a martyr in 101. However, the accounts of his martyrdom are legendary, composed about the fourth or fifth century. Probably the Basilica of St. Clement in Rome, one of the earliest parish churches of that city, is built on the site of Clement's home. Clement's First Epistle to the Corinthians (not to be confused with the writer now called Pseudo-Clement) was preserved and widely read in the early Church. It is a letter from the Church of Rome, authored by Clement, to the Church in Corinth, concerning a split that alienated a large number of the laity from the clergy. Clement deplores the unauthorized and un- justifiable division in the Corinthian Church and urges unity. He cites the cause of the quarrel as "envy and jealousy."

COMMENT: Clement urges charity (Ch. 49) to heal the division in the Church of Corinth, for "without charity, nothing is pleasing to God." Since Vatican II the entire Church is experiencing a polarization between the *old* and *new*. May we modern Christians take to heart the exhortation of Clement, imple- menting these words of St. Paul: "But above all these things have charity, which is the bond of perfection" (Col. 3-14).

QUOTE: "Charity unites us to God. . . .There is nothing mean in charity, nothing arrogant. Charity knows no schism, does not rebel, does all things in concord. In charity all the elect of God have been made perfect" *(First Epistle to the Corinthians,* Chapter 49).

November 23   *Optional*

COLUMBAN, abbot
(543?-615)

Columban was the greatest of the Irish mission- aries who worked on the European continent. As a young man he was greatly tormented by temptations of the flesh, and sought the advice of a religious woman who had lived a hermit's life for years. He saw in her answer a call to leave the world. He went first to a monk on an island in Lough Erne, then to the great monastic seat of learning at Bangor.

After many years of seclusion and prayer, he traveled to Gaul with 12 companion missionaries. They won wide respect for the rigor of their discipline, their preaching, and their commitment to charity and religious life in a time characterized by clerical slackness and civil strife. Columban established several monastaries in Europe which became centers of religion and culture.

Like all saints, he met opposition. Ultimately he had to appeal to the pope against complaints of Frankish bishops, for vindication of his orthodoxy and approval of Irish customs. He reproved the king for his licentious life, insisting that he marry. Since this threatened the power of the queen mother, Columban was ordered deported back to Ireland. His ship ran aground in a storm, and he continued his work in Europe, ultimately arriving in Italy, where he found favor with the king of the Lombards. In his last years he established the famous monastery of Bobbio, where he died. His writings include a treatise on penance and against Arianism, sermons, poetry and his monastic rule.

COMMENT: Now that public sexual license is approaching its extreme, we need the Church's jolting memory of a young man as concerned about chastity as Columban. And now that the comfort-captured Western world stands in tragic contrast to starving millions, we need the challenge to austerity and discipline of a group of Irish monks. They were too strict, we say; they went too far. How far shall *we* go?

QUOTE: Writing to the pope about a doctrinal controversy in Lombardy, Columban said: "We Irish, living in the farthest parts of the earth, are followers of St. Peter and St. Paul and of the disciples who wrote down the sacred canon under the Holy Spirit. We accept nothing outside this evangelical and apostolic teaching . . . . I confess I am grieved by the bad repute of the chair of St. Peter in this country . . . . Though Rome is great and known afar, she is great and honored with us only because of this chair . . . . Look after the peace of the Church, stand between your sheep and the wolves."

November 30   *Feast*

ANDREW, apostle

Andrew was St. Peter's brother, and was called with him. "As Jesus was walking along the sea of Galilee he watched two brothers, Simon now known as Peter, and his brother Andrew, casting a net into the sea. They were fishermen. He said to them, 'Come after me and I will make you fishers of men.' They immediately abandoned their nets and became his followers."

John the Evangelist presents Andrew as a disciple of John the Baptist. When Jesus walked by one day, John said, "Behold the lamb of God." Andrew and another disciple followed Jesus. He turned around and "noticed them following him. He asked them, 'What are you looking for?' They said to him, 'Rabbi, where do you stay?' He answered, 'Come and see.' So they went to see where he was lodged, and stayed with him that day."

Little else is said about Andrew in the Gospels. Before the multiplication of the loaves, it was Andrew who spoke up about the boy who had the barley loaves and fishes. When the gentiles went to see Jesus, they came to Philip. But Philip then had recourse to Andrew.

Legend has it that Andrew preached the Good News in what is now modern Greece and Turkey, and was crucified at Patras.

COMMENT: As in the case of all the apostles except Peter and John, the Gospels give us little about the holiness of Andrew. He was an apostle. That is enough. He was called personally by Jesus to proclaim the Good News, to heal with his power, to share his life and death. Holiness today is no different. It is a gift that includes a call to be concerned about the kingdom, an outgoing attitude that wants nothing more than to share the riches of Christ with all men.

STORY: "The Twelve assembled the community of the disciples and said, 'It is not right for us to neglect the word of God in order to wait on tables. Look around among your own number, brothers, for seven men acknowledged to be deeply spiritual and prudent, and we shall appoint them to this task. This will permit us to concentrate on prayer and the ministry of the word" (Acts 6,2-4).

FRANCIS XAVIER, priest
(1506-1552)

"What profit is it to a man if he gain the whole world, and lose his soul?" The words were repeated to a young teacher of philosophy who had a highly promising career in academics, with success and a life of prestige and honor before him.

Francis Xavier, 24 at the time, and living and teaching in Paris, did not heed these words at once. They came from a good friend, Ignatius of Loyola, whose tireless persuasion finally won the young man to Christ. Francis then made the spiritual exercises under the direction of Ignatius, and in 1534 joined his little community (the infant Society of Jesus). Together at Montmartre they vowed poverty, chastity and apostolic service, according to the directions of the pope.

From Venice, where he was ordained priest in 1537, he went on to Lisbon and from there sailed to the East Indies, landing at Goa, on the west coast of India. For the next 10 years he labored to bring the faith to such widely scattered peoples as the Hindus, the Malayans and the Japanese.

Wherever he went, he lived with the poorest people, sharing their food and rough accommodations. He spent countless hours ministering to the sick and the poor, particularly to lepers. Very often he had no time to sleep or even to say his breviary; but as we know from his letters he was filled always with God's presence and joy.

Francis went through the islands of Malaysia, then up to Japan. He learned enough Japanese to preach to simple folk, to instruct, and to baptize, and to establish missions for those who were to follow him. From Japan he had dreams of going to China, but this plan was never realized. Before reaching the mainland he died.

COMMENT: All of us are called to "go and preach to all nations." Our preaching is not necessarily on distant shores but to our families, our children, our husband or wife, fellow employees. And to preach, not with words, but by our everyday lives. Only by sacrifice, the giving up of all selfish gain, could Francis be free to bear the Good News to the world. Sacrifice is leaving yourself behind at times, for a greater good. The good of prayer, the good of helping someone in need, the good of just listening to another. The greatest gift we have is our time. Francis gave it to others.

STORY: Francis died on the island of Sancian, a hundred miles southwest of Hong Kong. In his final sickness he had to be removed from the ship because the Portuguese sailors feared that kindness to him would offend their master. They were forced to leave him on the sands of the shore, exposed to a bitter wind, but a Portuguese merchant led him into a ramshackle hut. He prayed continually, between spasms of delirium and the doubtful therapy of bleeding. He grew weaker and weaker. "I (Anthony, his friend) could see that he was dying, and put a lighted candle in his hand. Then, with the name of Jesus on his lips, he gave his spirit to his Creator and

Lord with great peace and repose."

JOHN DAMASCENE, priest and doctor
(676?-749?)

John spent most of his life in the monastery of St. Sabas, near Jerusalem, and all of his life under Moslem rule, indeed, protected by it. He was born in Damascus, received a classical and theological education, and followed his father in a government position under the Arabs. After a few years he resigned and went to the monastery of St. Sabas.

He is famous in three areas. First, he is known for his writings against the Iconoclasts, who opposed the veneration of images. Paradoxically, it was the Eastern Christian Emperor Leo who forbade the practice, and it was because John lived in Moslem territory that his enemies could not injure him. Second, he is famous for his treatise, *Exposition of the Orthodox Faith,* a summary of the Greek Fathers (of which he became the last). It is said that this book is to Eastern schools what the *Summa* of Aquinas became to the West. Thirdly, he is known as a poet, one of the two greatest of the Eastern Church, the other being Romanus the Melodist. His devotion to the Blessed Mother and his sermons on her feasts are well known.

COMMENT: John defended the Church's understanding of the veneration of images and explained the faith of the Church in several other controversies. For over 30 years he combined a life of prayer with these defenses and his other writings. His holiness expressed itself in putting his literary and preaching talents at the service of the Lord.

QUOTE: "The saints must be honored as friends of Christ and children and heirs of God, as John the theologian and evangelist says: 'But as many as received him, he gave them the power to be made the sons of God . . . .' Let us carefully observe the manner of life of all the apostles, martyrs, ascetics and just men who announced the coming of the Lord. And let us emulate their faith, charity, hope, zeal, life, patience under suffering, and perseverance unto death, so that we may also share their crowns of glory (*Exposition of the Orthodox Faith*, Book 4).

December 6   *Optional*

NICHOLAS, bishop
(d.350?)

The absence of the "hard facts" of history is not necessarily an obstacle to the popularity of saints, as the devotion to St. Nicholas shows. Both the Eastern and Western Churches honor him, and it is claimed that, after the Blessed Virgin, he is the saint most pictured by Christian artists. And yet, historically, we can pinpoint only the fact that Nicholas was the fourth-century bishop of Myra, a city in Lycia, a province of Asia Minor.

As with many of the saints, however, we are able to capture the relationship which Nicholas had with

God through the admiration which Christians have had for him — an admiration expressed in the colorful stories which have been told and retold through the centuries.

Perhaps the best-known story about Nicholas concerns his charity toward a poor man who was unable to provide dowries for his three daughters of marriageable age. Rather than see them forced to prostitution, Nicholas secretly tossed a bag of gold through the poor man's window on three separate occasions, thus enabling the daughters to be married. Over the centuries, this particular legend evolved into the custom of gift-giving on the saint's feast; and in the English-speaking countries, St. Nicholas became, by a twist of the tongue, Santa Claus — further expanding the example of generosity portrayed by this holy bishop.

COMMENT: The critical eye of modern history makes us take a deeper look at the legends surrounding St. Nicholas. But perhaps we can utilize the lesson taught by his legendary charity, and look deeper at our approach to material goods in the Christmas season, and seek ways to extend our sharing to those in real need.

QUOTE: "In order to be able to consult more suitably the welfare of the faithful according to the condition of each one, a bishop should strive to become duly acquainted with their needs in the social circumstances in which they live . . . . He should manifest his concern for all, no matter what their age, condition, or nationality, be they natives, strangers, or foreigners" (Vatican II, Bishops, 16).

AMBROSE, bishop and doctor
(340?-397)

One of Ambrose's biographers observed that at the Last Judgment men would still be divided between those who admired Ambrose and those who heartily disliked him. He emerges as the man of action who cut a furrow through the lives of his contemporaries. Even royal personages were numbered among those who were to suffer crushing divine punishments for standing in Ambrose's way.

When the Empress Justina attempted to wrest two basilicas from Ambrose's Catholics and give them to the Arians, he dared the eunuchs of the court to execute him. His own people rallied behind him in the face of imperial troops. In the midst of riots he both spurred and calmed his people with bewitching new hymns set to exciting Eastern melodies.

In his disputes with the Emperor Auxentius, he coined the principle: "The Emperor is in the Church, not above the Church." He publicly admonished Emperor Theodosius for the massacre of seven thousand innocent people. The emperor did public penance for his crime. This was Ambrose, the fighter, sent to Milan as Roman governor and chosen while yet a catechumen to be the people's bishop.

There is yet another side to Ambrose which influenced Augustine. Ambrose was a passionate little man with a high forehead, a long melancholy face and great eyes. We can picture him as a frail figure clasping the codex of Sacred Scripture. This was the Ambrose of aristocratic heritage and learning.

Augustine found the oratory of Ambrose less soothing and entertaining but far more learned than that of other contemporaries. Ambrose's sermons were often modeled on Cicero and his ideas betrayed the influence of contemporary thinkers and philosophers. He had no scruples in borrowing at length from pagan authors. He gloried in the pulpit in his ability to parade his spoils, "gold of the Egyptians," taken over from the pagan philosophers.

His sermons, his writings and his personal life reveal him as an "other-worldly" man involved in the great issues of his day. Man, for Ambrose, was above all his spirit. In order to rightly think of God and the human soul, the closest thing to God, no material reality at all was to be dwelt upon. He was an enthusiastic champion of consecrated virginity.

The influence of Ambrose on Augustine will always be open for discussion. The *Confessions* reveal some manly brusque encounters between Ambrose and Augustine, but there can be no doubt of Augustine's profound esteem for the learned bishop.

Neither is there any doubt that Monica loved Ambrose as an angel of God who had uprooted her son from his former ways and led him to his convictions about Christ. It was Ambrose, after all, who placed his hands on the shoulders of the naked Augustine as he descended into the baptismal fountain to put on Christ.

COMMENT: Ambrose exemplifies for us the truly catholic character of Christianity. He is a man steeped in the learning, law and culture of the ancients and his contemporaries. Yet, in the midst of active involvement in this world, this thought runs through Ambrose's life and preaching: the hidden meaning of the Scriptures calls our spirit to rise to another world.

QUOTE: "Man is not wrong when he regards himself as superior to bodily concerns, and as more than a speck of nature or a nameless constituent of the city of man. For by his interior qualities he outstrips the whole sum of mere things . . . . Steeped in wisdom, man passes through visible realities to those which are unseen" (Vatican II, The Church Today, 14-15).

December 11   *Optional*

DAMASUS, pope
(305?-384)

To his secretary St. Jerome, Damasus was "an incomparable person, learned in the Scriptures, a virgin doctor of the virgin Church, who loved chastity and heard its praises with pleasure."

Damasus seldom heard such unrestrained praise. Internal political struggles, doctrinal heresies, uneasy relations with his fellow bishops and those of the Eastern Church marred the peace of his pontificate.

The son of a Roman priest, possibly of Spanish extraction, Damasus started as a deacon in his father's church, and rose to priest of what later became the basilica of San Lorenzo in Rome. He served Pope Liberius (352-366) and followed him into exile.

When Liberius died, Damasus was elected bishop of Rome; but a minority elected and consecrated another deacon, Ursinus, as pope. The controversy between Damasus and the antipope resulted in violent battles in two basilicas, scandalizing the bishops of Italy. At the synod Damasus called on the occasion of his birthday, he asked them to approve his actions. The bishops' reply was curt: We assembled for a birthday, not to condemn a man unheard. Supporters of the antipope even managed to get Damasus accused of a grave crime — probably incontinence or adultery — as late as 378 A.D. He had to clear himself before both a civil court and a Church synod.

As Pope his lifestyle was simple in contrast to other ecclesiastics of Rome, and he was fierce in his denunciation of Arianism and other heresies. A misunderstanding of the Trinitarian terminology used by Rome threatened amicable relations with the Eastern Church, and Damasus was only moderately successful in dealing with the situation.

It was during his pontificate (380) that Christianity was declared the official religion of the Roman state, and Latin became the principal liturgical language as part of the Pope's reforms. His encouragement of St. Jerome's biblical studies led to the Vulgate, the Latin translation of Scripture which the Council of Trent (11 centuries later) declared to be "authentic in public readings, disputations, preachings."

COMMENTS: The history of the papacy and Church is inextricably mixed with the personal

171

biography of Damasus. In a troubled and pivotal period of Church history, he stands forth as a zealous defender of the faith, who knew when to be progressive and when to intrench.

Damasus makes us aware of two qualities of good leadership: alertness to the promptings of the Spirit, and service. His struggles are a reminder that Jesus never promised his Rock protection from hurricane winds nor his followers immunity from difficulties. His guarantee is final victory for fidelity to his Spirit.

QUOTE: An act of faith: "He who walking on the sea could calm the bitter waves, who gives life to the dying seeds of the earth; he who was able to loose the mortal chains of death, and after three days' darkness could bring again to the upper world the brother for his sister Martha: he, I believe, will make Damasus rise again from the dust" (epitaph Damasus wrote for himself).

December 12   *Optional*

JANE FRANCES de CHANTAL, religious
(1562-1641)

Jane Frances was wife, mother, nun and founder of a religious community. Her mother died when she was 18 months old, and her father, head of parliament at Dijon, France, became the main influence on her education. She developed into a woman of beauty and refinement, lively and cheerful in temperament. At 21 she married Baron de Chantal, by

172

whom she had six children, three of whom died in infancy. At her castle residence she restored the custom of daily Mass, and was seriously engaged in various charitable works. Her husband was killed after seven years of marriage, and she sank into deep dejection for four months at her family home. Her father-in-law threatened to disinherit her children if she did not return to his home. He was then 75, vain, fierce, and extravagant. Jane Frances managed to remain cheerful in spite of him and his insolent housekeeper.

When she was 32 she met St. Francis de Sales, who became her spiritual director, softening some of the severities imposed by her former director. She wanted to become a nun, but he persuaded her to defer this decision. She took a vow to remain unmarried and to obey her director.

After three years Francis told her of his plan to found an institute of women which would be a haven for those whose health, age or other considerations barred them from entering the already established orders. There would be no cloister, and they would be free to undertake spiritual and corporal works of mercy. They were primarily intended to exemplify the virtues of Mary at the Visitation (hence their name, the Visitation nuns), humility and meekness.

The usual opposition arose and Francis de Sales was obliged to make it a cloistered community, with the rule of St. Augustine. Francis wrote his famous *Treatise on the Love of God* for them. The congregation (three women) began when Jane Frances was 45. She underwent great sufferings: Francis de Sales died, her son was killed, a plague ravaged France, her daughter-in-law and son-in-law died. She whipped up the local authorities to great efforts for the victims of the plague and put all the resources of her convent at the disposal of the sick.

During a part of her religious life she had to undergo great trials of the spirit — interior anguish, darkness and spiritual dryness. She died while on a visitation of convents of the community.

COMMENT: It may strike some of us as unusual that a saint should be subject to spiritual dryness, darkness, interior anguish. We tend to think that such things are the usual condition of "ordinary" sinful people. Some of our lack of spiritual liveliness may indeed be our fault. But the life of faith is still one that is lived in trust, and sometimes the darkness is so great that trust is pressed to its limit.

QUOTE: St. Vincent de Paul said of Jane Frances: "She was full of faith, yet all her life had been tormented by thoughts against it. While apparently enjoying the peace and easiness of mind of souls who have reached a high state of virtue, she suffered such interior trials that she often told me her mind was so filled with all sorts of temptations and abominations that she had to strive not to look within herself . . . . But for all that suffering her face never lost its serenity, nor did she once relax in the fidelity God asked of her. And so I regard her as one of the holiest souls I have ever met on this earth" (Butler's *Lives of the Saints*).

LUCY, virgin and martyr

Every little girl named Lucy must bite her tongue in disappointment when she first tries to find out what there is to know about her patron saint. The older books will have a lengthy paragraph detailing a small number of traditions. Newer books will have a lengthy paragraph showing that there is little basis in history for these traditions. The single fact survives that a disappointed suitor accused Lucy of being a Christian and she was executed in Syracuse of Sicily in the year 304. But it is also true that her name is mentioned in the Roman canon of the Mass; geographical places are named after her; a popular song has her name as its title; and down through the centuries many thousands of little girls were proud of the name Lucy.

One can easily imagine what a young Christian woman had to contend with in pagan Sicily of the year 300. If you have trouble imagining, just glance at the pagan world around you today and the barriers it presents against leading a good Christian life.

Her friends wondered aloud about this hero of Lucy's, an obscure itinerant preacher in a far off captive nation that was destroyed more than 200 years before. Once a carpenter, he had been crucified by the Roman soldiers after his own people sentenced him to death. Lucy believed with her whole soul that this man had risen from the dead. Heaven had put a stamp on all he said and did. To give witness to her faith she had made a vow of virginity.

What a hubbub this caused among her pagan friends. The kindlier ones just thought her a little strange. To be pure before marriage was an ancient Roman ideal, rarely found but not to be condemned. To exclude marriage altogether, however, that was too much. She must have something sinister to hide, the tongues wagged.

Lucy knew of the heroism of earlier virgin martyrs. She remained faithful to their example and to the example of the Carpenter, whom she knew to be the Son of God.

COMMENT: If you are a little girl named Lucy, you need not bite your tongue in disappointment. Your patron is a genuine, authentic heroine, first class, an abiding inspiration for you and for all Christians. The moral courage of the young Sicilian martyr shines forth as a guiding light, just as bright for today's youth as it was in 304 A.D.

QUOTE: "The Gospel tells us of all that Jesus suffered, of the insults that fell upon him. But, from Bethlehem to Calvary, the brilliance that radiates from his divine purity spread more and more and won over the crowds. So great was the austerity and the enchantment of his conduct.

"So may it be with you, beloved daughters. Blessed be the discretion, the mortifications and the renouncements with which you seek to render this virtue more brilliant .... May your conduct prove to all that chastity is not only a possible virtue but a social virtue, which must be strongly defended through prayer, vigilance and the mortification of the senses" (Pope John XXIII, *Il Tempio Massimo*, Letter to Women Religious).

JOHN OF THE CROSS, priest and doctor
(1542-1591)

John is a saint, because his life was an heroic effort to live up to his name: "of the Cross." The foolishness of the cross came to full realization in time. "If anyone wishes to follow me, let him deny himself, take up his cross daily" is the story of John's life. The Paschal Mystery — through death to life — strongly marks John as reformer, mystic-poet and theologian-priest.

Ordained a Carmelite priest at 25 (1567), John met Teresa of Avila and like her vowed himself to the primitive rule of the Carmelites. As partner with Teresa, and in his own right, John engaged in the work of reform, and came to experience the price of reform: increasing opposition, misunderstanding, persecution, imprisonment. He came to know the cross acutely — to experience the dying of Jesus — as he sat month after month in his dark, damp, narrow cell with only his God!

Yet, the paradox! In this dying of imprisonment John came to life, uttering poetry. In the darkness of the dungeon, John's spirit came into the Light. There are many mystics, many poets; John is unique as mystic-poet, expressing in his prison-cross the ecstasy of mystical union with God in the *Spiritual Canticle.*

But, as agony leads to ecstasy, so John had his *Ascent to Mt. Carmel.* As man-Christian-Carmelite, he experienced in himself this purifying ascent; as spiritual director, he sensed it in others; as psychologist-theologian, he described and analyzed it in his prose writings. His prose works are outstanding in underscoring the cost of discipleship, the path to union with God: rigorous discipline, abandonment, purification. Uniquely and strongly John underlines the Gospel paradox: the cross leads to resurrection, agony to ecstasy, darkness to light, abandonment to possession, denial of self to union with God. If you want to save your life, you must lose it. John is truly "of the Cross." He died at 49 — a life short, but full.

COMMENT: John in his life and writings has a crucial word for us today. We tend to be rich, soft, comfortable. We shrink even from words like self-denial, mortification, purification, asceticism, discipline. We run from the cross. John's message — like the Gospel — is loud and clear: DON'T — if you really want to live!

QUOTE: Thomas Merton said of John: "Just as we can never separate asceticism from mysticism, so in St. John of the Cross we find darkness and light, suffering and joy, sacrifice and love united together so closely that they seem at times to be identified."
     In John's words:
Never was fount so clear,
   undimmed and bright;
From it alone, I know, proceeds all light,
   although 'tis night.

PETER CANISIUS, priest and doctor
(1521-1597)

The energetic life of Peter Canisius should demolish any stereotypes we may have of the life of a saint as dull or routine. Peter lived his 76 years at a pace which cannot but be considered heroic, even in our time of rapid change and future shock. A man blessed with many talents, Peter is an excellent example of the scriptural man who develops his talents for the sake of the Lord's work.

He was one of the most important figures in the Catholic Counter-Reformation in Germany. His was such a key role that he has often been called the "Second Apostle of Germany," in that his life parallels the earlier work of Boniface.

Although Peter once accused himself of idleness in his youth, he could not have been idle too long, for at the age of 19 he received a master's degree from the university at Cologne. Soon afterwards he met Peter Faber, the first disciple of Ignatius Loyola, who influenced him so much that he joined the recently formed Society of Jesus.

At this early age Peter had already taken up a practice he continued throughout his life — a process of study, reflection, prayer and writing. After his ordination in 1546, he became widely known for his editions of the works of St. Cyril of Alexandria and St. Leo the Great. Besides this reflective literary bent, Peter had a zeal for the apostolate. He could often be found visiting the sick or prisoners, even when his assigned duties in other areas were more than enough to keep most men fully occupied.

In 1547 Peter attended several sessions of the Council of Trent, whose decrees he was later assigned to implement. After a brief teaching assignment at the Jesuit college at Messina, Peter was entrusted with the mission to Germany — from that point on his life's work. He taught in several universities and was instrumental in establishing many colleges and seminaries. He wrote a catechism which explained the Catholic faith in a way which common people could understand — a great need of that age.

Renowned as a popular preacher, Peter packed churches with those eager to hear his eloquent proclamation of the Gospel. He had great diplomatic ability, often serving as a reconciler between disputing factions. In his letters (filling eight volumes) one finds words of wisdom and counsel to people in all walks of life. At times he wrote unprecedented letters of criticism to leaders of the Church — yet always in the context of a loving, sympathetic concern.

At 70 Peter suffered a paralytic seizure, but he continued to preach and write with the aid of a secretary until his death on December 21, 1597.

COMMENT: Peter's untiring efforts are an apt example for those involved in the renewal of the Church or the growth of moral consciousness in business or government. He is regarded as one of the creators of the Catholic press, and can easily be a model for the Christian author or journalist. Teachers can see in his life a passion for the transmission of truth. Whether we have much to give, as Peter Canisius did, or whether we have only a little to give, as did the poor widow in the Gospel, the important thing is to give our all. It is in this way that Peter is so exemplary for Christians in an age of rapid change when we are called to be in the world but not of the world.

QUOTE: When asked if he felt overworked, Peter replied "If you have too much to do, with God's help you will find time to do it all."

December 23   *Optional*

JOHN OF KANTY, priest
(1390?-1473)

John was a country lad who made good in the big city and the big university of Krakow in Poland. After brilliant studies he was ordained a priest and became a professor of theology. The inevitable opposition which saints encounter led to his being ousted by rivals and sent to be a parish priest at Olkusz. An extremely humble man, he did his best, but his best was not to the liking of his parishioners. Besides, he was afraid of the responsibilities of his position. But in the end he won his people's hearts. After some time he returned to Krakow and taught Sacred Scripture for the remainder of his life.

He was a serious man, and humble, but known to all the poor of Krakow for his kindness. His goods and his money were always at their disposal, and time and again they took advantage of him. He kept only the money and clothes absolutely needed to support himself. He slept little, and then on the floor, ate sparingly, and took no meat. He made a pilgrimage to Jerusalem, hoping to be martyred by the Turks. He made four pilgrimages to Rome, carrying his luggage on his back. When he was warned to look after his health, he was quick to point out that, for all their austerity, the fathers of the desert lived remarkably long lives.

COMMENT: John of Kanty is a typical saint: he was kind, humble and generous, he suffered opposition, and led an austere, penitential life. Most Christians in an affluent society can understand all the ingredients but the last: anything more than mild self-discipline seems reserved for athletes and ballet dancers. Christmas is a good time at least to reject self-indulgence.

STORY: The Second Nocturn of this feast in the old breviary included this story. He was once accosted by robbers, who took his money. They asked if he had any more, and he replied in the negative. When they had gone, he discovered some coins sewn in his cloak, ran after the robbers, shouted for them to stop, and gave them the coins. They were so amazed that they gave back what they had taken.

STEPHEN, first martyr
(d. 36?)

All we know of Stephen is found in chapters 6

and 7 of the Acts of the Apostles. It is enough to tell us what kind of man he was.

"The number of Christians was growing. Those who spoke Greek complained that their widows were being neglected in the daily distribution of food, as compared with the widows of those who spoke Hebrew. The apostles could not neglect the word of God to serve tables, so they asked the community to choose seven prudent and deeply spiritual men. Among those selected was Stephen, a man filled with faith and the Holy Spirit."

Acts says that Stephen was a man filled with grace and power, who worked great wonders among the people. Certain Jews, members of the "Synagogue of Roman Freedmen," debated with Stephen, but proved no match for the wisdom and Spirit with which he spoke. They persuaded others to make the charge of blasphemy against him. He was seized and carried before the Sandedrin.

In his speech, Stephen recalled the guidance of God through Israel's history, as well as Israel's idolatry and disobedience. He then claimed that his persecutors were showing this same spirit. "You are always opposing the Holy Spirit, just as your fathers did before you."

His speech brought anger from the crowd. But "Stephen, meanwhile, filled with the Holy Spirit, looked to the sky and saw the glory of God, and Jesus standing at God's right hand. 'Look!' he exclaimed, 'I see an opening in the sky, and the Son of Man standing at God's right hand.' They dragged him out of the city and stoned him to death. As he was being killed, he prayed, 'Lord Jesus, receive my

spirit . . . . Lord, do not hold this sin against them.' "

COMMENT: Stephen died as Jesus did: falsely accused, brought to unjust condemnation because he spoke the truth fearlessly. He died with his eyes trustfully fixed on God; and with a prayer of forgiveness on his lips. A "happy" death is one that finds us in the same spirit, whether our dying is as quiet as Joseph's or as violent as Stephen's: courage, total trust, and forgiving love.

STORY: "The witnesses meantime were piling their

cloaks at the feet of a young man named Saul, who for his part concurred in the act of killing . . . . After that, Saul began to harass the Church. He entered house after house, dragged men and women out, and threw them in jail . . . . Still breathing murderous threats against the Lord's disciples . . . as he traveled along and was approaching Damascus, a light from the sky suddenly flashed about him, he fell to the ground and at the same time heard a voice saying, 'Saul, Saul, why do you persecute me?' 'Who are you, sir?' he asked. The voice answered, 'I am Jesus, whom you are persecuting'" (Acts 7,58;8,1.3;9,1.3-5).

December 27   *Feast*

JOHN, apostle and evangelist

It is God who calls; man answers. The vocation of John and his brother James is stated very simply in the Gospels, along with that of Peter and his brother Andrew: Jesus called them; they followed. The absoluteness of their response is indicated by the account. James and John were in a boat with their father Zebedee, mending their nets. "Immediately he called them. And they left their father Zebedee in the boat, with the hired men, and followed him."

That faith was to be rewarded by a special friendship with Jesus for the three former fishermen — Peter, James and John. They alone were privileged to be present at the Transfiguration, the raising of the daughter of Jairus, and the agony in

185

Gethsemane. But John's friendship was even more special. His own Gospel refers to him as "the disciple whom Jesus loved," the one who reclined next to Jesus at the Last Supper, and the one to whom he gave the exquisite honor, as he stood beneath the cross, of caring for his mother. "Son, behold your mother. Woman, behold your son."

Because of the depth of his Gospel, John is usually thought of as the eagle of theology, soaring in high regions that other writers did not enter. But the ever-frank Gospels reveal some very human traits. Jesus gave James and John the nickname, "sons of thunder." While it is difficult to know exactly what this meant, a clue is given in two incidents. They (another account says their mother) asked that they might sit in the places of honor in Jesus' kingdom — one on his right hand, one on his left. When Jesus asked them if they could drink the cup he would drink, and be baptized with his baptism of pain, they blithely answered, "We can!" Jesus said that they would indeed share his cup, but that sitting at his right hand was not his to give. It was for those to whom it had been reserved by the Father. The other apostles were indignant at the mistaken ambition of the brothers, and Jesus took the occasion to teach them the true nature of authority. "Anyone of you who aspires to greatness must serve the rest. Such is the case with the Son of Man, who has come, not to be served by others, but to serve, to give his own life as a ransom for the many."

On another occasion the "sons of thunder" asked Jesus if they should not call down fire from heaven upon the inhospitable Samaritans, who would not welcome Jesus because he was on his way to Jerusalem. But Jesus "turned to them only to reprimand them." On the first Easter, Magdalen "ran off to Peter and the other disciple (the one Jesus loved) and told them, 'They have taken the Lord from the tomb. We don't know where they have put him." John recalls, perhaps with a smile, that he and Peter "were running side by side, but then "the other apostle outran Peter and reached the tomb first." He did not enter, but waited for Peter and let him go in first. "Then the disciple who had arrived first went in. He saw and believed."

John is with Peter when the first great miracle after the resurrection took place — the cure of the man crippled from birth, which led to their spending the night in jail together. The mysterious experience of the resurrection is perhaps best contained in the words of Acts: "Observing the self-assurance of Peter and John, and recognizing that the speakers were uneducated men of no standing, the questioners were amazed. Then they recognized these men as having been with Jesus" (Acts 3,13).

John is of course best known for his great Gospel, the letters, and the Book of Revelation. His Gospel is a very personal account. He sees the glorious and divine Jesus already in the incidents of his mortal life. At the Last Supper, Jesus speaks in John's Gospel as if he were already in heaven It is the Gospel of Jesus' glory.

COMMENT: It is a long way from being eager to sit on a throne of power, to call down fire from heaven, to becoming the man who could write: "The way we come to understand love is that he laid down his life for us. We must lay down our lives for our brothers."

QUOTE: A persistent story has it that John's "parishioners" grew tired of his one sermon, which relentlessly emphasized: "Love one another." Whether the story is true or not, it has basis in John's writing. He wrote what may be called a summary of the Bible: "We have come to know and to believe in the love God has for us. God is love, and he who abides in love abides in God and God in him."

December 29   *Optional*
THOMAS BECKET, bishop and martyr
(1118-1170)

A strong man who wavered for a moment, but then learned one cannot come to terms with evil, and so became a strong churchman, a martyr, a saint — that was Thomas a Becket, Archbishop of Canterbury, murdered in his cathedral December 29, 1170.

His career had been a stormy one. While archdeacon of Canterbury, he was made chancellor of England at the age of 36 by his friend King Henry II. When Henry felt it advantageous to raise his chancellor to the archbishopric of Canterbury, Thomas gave him fair warning: he might not accept all of Henry's intrusions into Church affairs. Nevertheless, he was made archbishop (1162), resigned his chancellorship, and reformed his whole way of life!

Troubles began. Henry insisted upon usurping Church rights. At one time, supposing some conciliatory action possible, Thomas came close to compromise. He momentarily approved the Constitutions of Clarendon which would have denied the clergy the right of trial by a Church court and prevented them from making direct appeal to Rome. But Thomas rejected the Constitutions, fled to France for safety, and remained in exile for seven years. When he returned to England he suspected it would mean certain death. Because Thomas refused to remit censures he had placed upon bishops favored by the king, Henry cried out in a rage, "Will no one rid me of this troublesome priest!" Four knights, taking his words as his wish, slew Thomas in the Canterbury cathedral.

Within three years he was a saint of the Church and his tomb a shrine of pilgrimage. Henry II himself did penance at Thomas' tomb, but a later Henry (VIII) despoiled that tomb and scattered the saint's relics. However, Thomas a Becket remains a hero-saint down to our own times.

COMMENT: No one becomes a saint without struggle, especially with himself. Thomas knew he must stand firm in defense of truth and right, even at the cost of his life. We also must take a stand in the face of pressures — against dishonesty, deceit, destruction of life — at the cost of popularity, convenience, promotion, and even greater goods.

QUOTE: In T.S. Eliot's drama, *Murder in the Cathedral*, Becket is faced by a final tempter to seek martyrdom for earthly glory and revenge. With real insight into his life situation, Thomas responds:

"The last temptation is the greatest treason:
To do the right deed for the wrong reason."

SYLVESTER I, pope
(d.335)

When you think of this pope, you think of the Edict of Milan, the emergence of the Church from the catacombs, the building of the great basilicas, Saint John Lateran, Saint Peter's and others, the Council of Nicaea and other critical events. But for the most part, these events were planned or brought about by the Emperor Constantine.

A great store of legends has grown up around the man who was pope at this most important time, but very little can be historically established. We know for sure that his papacy lasted from 314 until his death in 335. Reading between the lines of history, we are assured that no one but a very strong and wise man could have preserved the essential independence of the Church in the face of the overpowering figure of the Emperor Constantine. The bishops in general remained loyal to the Holy See and at times expressed apologies to Sylvester for undertaking important ecclesiastical projects at the urging of Constantine.

COMMENT: It takes deep humility and courage in the face of criticism for a leader to stand aside and let events take their course, when asserting one's authority would only lead to useless tension and strife. Sylvester teaches a valuable lesson for Church leaders, politicians, parents and others in authority.

QUOTE: To emphasize the continuity of Holy Orders, the recent Roman breviary in its biographies of popes ends with important statistics. On the feast of Saint Sylvester it recounts: "He presided at seven December ordinations at which he created 42 priests, 25 deacons and 65 bishops for various sees." The Holy Father is indeed the heart of the Church's sacramental system, an essential element of its unity.

INDEX OF SAINTS

Bernard, Aug. 20, vol. II, p. 57.
Bernardine of Siena, May 20, vol. I, p. 112.
Blase, Feb. 3, vol. I, p. 35.
Bonaventure, July 15, vol. II, p. 14.
Boniface, June 5, vol. I, p. 128.
Bridget, July 23, vol. II, p. 20.
Bruno, Oct. 6, vol. II, p. 106.

Cajetan, Aug. 7, vol. II, p. 40.
Callistus I, Oct. 14, vol. II, p. 111.
Camillus de Lellis, July 14, vol. II, p. 12.
Casimir, March 4, vol. I, p. 55.
Catherine of Siena, April 29, vol. I, p. 93.
Cecilia, Nov. 22, vol. II, p. 157.
Charles Borromeo, Nov. 4, vol. II, p. 138.
Charles Lwanga, June 3, vol. I, p. 126.
Clare, Aug. 11, vol. II, p. 47.
Clement I, Nov. 23, vol. II, p. 158.
Columban, Nov. 23, vol. II, p. 159.
Cornelius, Sept. 16, vol. II, p. 83.
Cosmas, Sept. 26, vol. II, p. 93.
Cyprian, Sept. 16, vol. II, p. 85.
Cyril, Feb. 14, vol. I, p. 45.
Cyril of Alexandria, June 27, vol. I, p. 150.
Cyril of Jerusalem, March 18, vol. I, p. 66.

Damasus, Dec. 11, vol. II, p. 170.
Damian, Sept. 26, vol. II, p. 93.
Denis, Oct. 9, vol. II, p. 108.
Dominic, Aug. 8, vol. II, p. 42.

Elizabeth Seton, Jan. 4, vol. I, p. 5.
Elizabeth of Hungary, Nov. 17, vol. II, p. 154.

Elizabeth of Portugal, July 4, vol. II, p. 3.
Ephrem, June 9, vol. I, p. 132.
Eusebius of Vercelli, Aug. 2, vol. II, p. 35.

Fabian, Jan. 20, vol. I, p. 16.
Felicity, March 7, vol. I, p. 57.
Fidelis of Sigmaringen, April 24, vol. I, p. 87.
Frances of Rome, March 9, vol. I, p. 61.
Frances Xavier Cabrini, Nov. 13, vol. II, p. 147.
Francis of Assisi, Oct. 4, vol. II, p. 102.
Francis of Paola, April 2, vol. I, p. 72.
Francis de Sales, Jan. 24, vol. I, p. 21.
Francis Xavier, Dec. 3, vol. II, p. 163.

George, April 23, vol. I, p. 86.
Gertrude, Nov. 16, vol. II, p. 153.
Gregory the Great, Sept. 3, vol. II, p. 75.
Gregory Nazianzen, Jan. 2, vol. I, p. 3.
Gregory VII, May 25, vol. I, p. 116.

Hedwig, Oct. 16, vol. II, p. 116.
Henry, July 13, vol. II, p. 11.   *Hippolytus 13 aug*
Hilary, Jan. 13, vol. I, p. 12.

Ignatius of Antioch, Oct. 17, vol. II, p. 120.
Ignatius Loyola, July 31, vol. II, p. 29.
Irenaeus, June 28, vol. I, p. 152.
Isaac Jogues, Oct. 19, vol. II, p. 123.
Isidore of Seville, April 4, vol. I, p. 75.
Isidore the Farmer, May 15, vol. I, p. 108.

James, apostle, July 25, vol. II, p. 21.
James, apostle, May 3, vol. I, p. 101.

Jane Frances de Chantal, Dec. 12, vol. II, p. 172.
Januarius, Sept. 19, vol. II, p. 90.
Jerome, Sept. 30, vol. II, p. 98.
Jerome Emiliani, Feb. 8, vol. I, p. 41.
John I, May 18, vol. I, p. 110.
John, apostle, Dec. 27, vol. II, p. 185.
John Baptist, birth, June 24, vol. I, p. 147.
John Baptist, beheading, Aug. 29, vol. II, p. 73.
John Baptist de la Salle, April 7, vol. I, p. 79.
John de Brebeuf, Oct. 19, vol. II, p. 125.
John Bosco, Jan. 31, vol. I, p. 33.
John of Capistrano, Oct. 23, vol. II, p. 129.
John Chrysostom, Sept. 13, vol. II, p. 80.
John of the Cross, Dec. 14, vol. II, p. 177.
John Damascene, Dec. 4, vol. II, p. 165.
John Eudes, Aug. 19, vol. II, p. 55.
John Fisher, June 22, vol. I, p. 143.
John of God, March 8, vol. I, p. 59.
John of Kanty, Dec. 23, vol. II, p. 181.
John Leonardi, Oct. 9, vol. II, p. 109.
John Neumann, Jan. 5, vol. I, p. 8.
John Vianney, Aug. 4, vol. II, p. 37.
Joachim, July 26, vol. II, p. 24.
Josaphat, Nov. 12, vol. II, p. 144.
Joseph, March 19, vol. I, p. 68.
Joseph the Worker, May 1, vol. I, p. 98.
Joseph Calasanz, Aug. 25, vol. II, p. 67.
Jude, Oct. 28, vol. II, p. 133.
Justin, June 1, vol. I, p. 124.

Lawrence, Aug. 10, vol. II, p. 45.
Lawrence Brindisi, July 21, vol. II, p. 16.
Leo the Great, Nov. 10, vol. II, p. 140.

Louis of France, Aug. 25, vol. II, p. 65.
Lucy, Dec. 13, vol. II, p. 175.
Luke, Oct. 18, vol. II, p. 121.

Marcellinus, June 2, vol. I, p. 125.
Margaret Mary Alacoque, Oct. 16, vol. II, p. 118.
Margaret of Scotland, Nov. 16, vol. II, p. 151.
Maria Goretti, July 6, vol. II, p. 7.
Mark, April 25, vol. I, p. 89.
Martha, July 29, vol. II, p. 25.
Martin I, April 13, vol. I, p. 82.
Martin de Porres, Nov. 3, vol. II, p. 135.
Martin of Tours, Nov. 11, vol. II, p. 142.
Mary Magdalen, July 22, vol. II, p. 18.
Mary Magdalen de Pazzi, May 25, vol. I, p. 117.
Matthew, Sept. 21, vol. II, p. 91.
Matthias, May 14, vol. I, p. 106.
Methodius, Feb. 14, vol. I, p. 45.
Monica, Aug. 27, vol. II, p. 69.

Nereus, May 12, vol. I, p. 104.
Nicholas, Dec. 6, Vol. II, p. 166.
Norbert, June 6, vol. I, p. 130.

Pancras, May 12, vol. I, p. 105.
Patrick, March 17, vol. I, p. 64.
Paul, apostle, June 29, vol. I, p. 156.
Paul, conversion, Jan. 25, vol. I, p. 23.
Paul of the Cross, Oct. 19, vol. II, p. 126.
Paul Miki, Feb. 5, vol. I, p. 39.
Paulinus of Nola, June 22, vol. I, p. 141.
Perpetua, March 7, vol. I, p. 57.
Peter, apostle, June 29, vol. I, p. 153.

Peter, chair of, Feb. 22, vol. I, p. 52.
Peter, martyr, June 2, vol. I, p. 125.
Peter Canisius, Dec. 21, vol. II, p. 179.
Peter Chanel, April 28, vol. I, p. 91.
Peter Chrysologus, July 30, vol. II, p. 28.
Peter Claver, Sept. 9, vol. II, p. 77.
Peter Damian, Feb. 21, vol. I, p. 49.
Philip, apostle, May 3, vol. I, p. 101.
Philip Neri, May 26, vol. I, p. 120.
Pius V, April 30, vol. I, p. 95.
Pius X, Aug. 21, vol. II, p. 59.
Polycarp, Feb. 23, vol. I, p. 54.
Pontian, Aug. 13, vol. II, p. 50.

Raymond of Penyafort, Jan. 7, vol. I, p. 10.
Robert Bellarmine, Sept. 17, vol. II, p. 87.
Romuald, June 19, vol. I, p. 138.
Rose of Lima, Aug. 23, vol. II, p. 61.

Scholastica, Feb. 10, vol. I, p. 43.
Sebastian, Jan. 20, vol. I, p. 17.
Seven Founders of Servites, Feb. 17, vol. I, p. 48.
Simon, apostle, Oct. 28, vol. II, p. 133.
Sixtus II, Aug. 7, vol. II, p. 39.
Stanislaus, April 11, vol. I, p. 81.
Stephen, Dec. 26, vol. II, p. 182.
Stephen of Hungary, Aug. 16, vol. II, p. 53.
Sylvester I, Dec. 31, vol. II, p. 190.

Teresa of Avila, Oct. 15, vol. II, p. 113.
Therese of the Child Jesus, Oct. 1, vol. II, p. 100.
Thomas, apostle, July 3, vol. II, p. 1.
Thomas Aquinas, Jan. 28, vol. I, p. 31.

Thomas Becket, Dec. 29, vol. II, p. 188.
Thomas More, June 22, vol. I, p. 145.
Timothy, Jan. 26, vol. I, p. 25.
Titus, Jan. 26, vol. I, p. 27.
Turibius of Mongrovejo, March 23, vol. I, p. 71.

Vincent, Jan. 22, vol. I, p. 19.
Vincent Ferrer, April 5, vol. I, p. 76.
Vincent de Paul, Sept. 27, vol. II, p. 94.

Wenceslaus, Sept. 28, vol. II, p. 96.